Going In Seine

Polly Fielding

ISBN-13: 978-1482609226

Also by Polly Fielding:

The 5:2 Diet Made eZy
(*A proven, painless way to lose weight*)

Missing Factor
(*A personal experience of haemophilia*)

And This Is My Adopted Daughter
(*The powerful true story of an adopted child's relationship with two mothers*)

A Mind To Be Free
(*The minefield of the mental health system*)

Available from Amazon

To Dennis, without whom…

Preface

All the events in this book actually happened. Not necessarily to me. But they happened.

Chapter *Un*

I need a toilet. And Paris is not the easiest place to find one.

I could, of course, go into a café. But then I'd be obliged to have a drink so that I could use their convenience. And less than two hours later I'd want to go again. It's a vicious circle.

If I could be like my husband Dennis I wouldn't have this problem. He uses the toilet only twice a day, or so he claims – I've never actually monitored his toilet habits.

"It's no good, I can't wait any longer. Let's go in here." Giving my daughter no time to argue I'm already diving into the nearest bar.

While Nikki orders I let instinct guide me to the toilet, a talent developed through years of trial and error worldwide. I've always had to pander to my weak bladder.

Oh no, it's one of those! A square ceramic basin set into the floor with ribbed tiles on either side requiring me to pee whilst squatting and making it difficult to avoid soaking my shoes. I perch precariously over the hole…

My mobile rings. How am I going to manage this? I can't leave it – but if I don't get it out of my pocket fast they'll ring off. It's obviously important and probably from England since nobody here knows my number. I nearly topple sideways in a frantic effort to get to my pocket, peeing on my jeans in the process…

"Yes?" I gasp breathlessly.

"I won't be long because this call is costing you as well as me…" Perhaps Dennis thinks he has to shout because of the distance.

"What's the matter? Why are you ringing me when I'm on the toilet?"

"When are you *not* on the loo? Listen. I've had an idea. Why don't we use our retirement savings to buy a flat in Paris?"

"I'm sorry, it's a bad line." I wonder if I sound as flustered as I feel. "It sounded like you said something about buying a flat in Paris." I'm struggling to pull up my knickers with one hand…

"That's exactly what I did say. You've always loved everything French and you've often said you wished you could live there. Also, Nikki would be sure of a roof over her head for a while, instead of hopping in and out of friends' flats…Hello? Are you still there?"

"Just about," I reply, bewildered. "I'm stunned into silence by your crazy idea. I'm here for two weeks, not two years."

"Well, it was only a suggestion." Dennis sounds defensive. "Love to Nikki. And enjoy the rest of your day."

I feel like he's just ruined it. I concentrate on trying to dry the wet patch on my jeans with a paper towel.

Dazed, I rejoin Nikki, sit sipping my hot chocolate, stare mindlessly out of the window trying to get my head round Dennis's call.

"What's up?" Nikki's voice jerks me back to the present. "You look miles away."

"You'll never believe it, your dad rang a

moment ago. He wants me to buy a flat in Paris."

"Why?"

"He says it would be somewhere we could visit and you could use till you get a place of your own." I wave my hand dismissively.

Nikki looks thoughtful. Hmmm, maybe I shouldn't have said anything...

My worst fear is confirmed when her face brightens.

"Hey, that's fantastic, Mum!"

"Hang on, I'm telling you what your dad said. I didn't say I agree with it. I don't even know anything about buying property abroad. We're talking about buying a flat, not a baguette."

"I know that. But some of my French friends have got apartments and they can advise us." She's beginning to sound a bit too enthusiastic for my liking. "Let's at least look," she argues, with that persuasive expression on her face. She knows I'll give in – she knows which buttons to push.

Before I realise what's happening I'm being steered towards the nearest estate agent. Whatever happened to my relaxing fortnight helping Nikki to cat-sit for a friend? Three weeks ago I was in a psychiatric hospital, recovering from a nervous breakdown. Now I'm about to look for a flat in Paris…

I *must* be mad!

The young man seated behind the desk rises instantly to his feet as we approach him. He smiles, his gaze lingering on my pretty daughter, before gesturing to a couple of seats facing him. I sink back into the comfortable leather upholstery, leaving Nikki, who is already fluent in the language, to do the talking. My own French is adequate for small talk but certainly not for negotiations of this kind. I hope one day I'll regain the fluency I had when, at the age of twenty-three, I was a nanny in the south of France.

Perhaps Dennis' idea isn't completely crazy. I can imagine friends asking what I'm up to and me replying casually, "Oh, we're just popping over to Paris for a few days." Sounds rather more interesting than, "We're doing a spot of gardening," or, "We're having lunch at the Age Concern Centre…"

"Mum..." Nikki's insistent tone brings me back to reality. "He wants to know what sort of price we're prepared to pay. I've already told him we want a two-roomed place in central Paris."

Wait a minute, I think defensively. What's this about "we"? And when did "we" discuss the location and number of rooms?

"Nikki, we've got an absolute limit of forty-two thousand pounds and even that's pushing it."

She asks the agent for the use of his calculator.

"That's roughly sixty-two thousand Euros," she reads out.

"Yes and not a penny more."

A further brief discussion follows, during which I'm sure that we'll be politely but firmly ushered out of the office.

But no – Nikki turns to me excitedly. "He says he has exactly the right apartment for us. It works out at forty-four thousand pounds and it's bang in the heart of the city. And what's more, he's willing to drive us there right now," she says without pausing for breath.

I feel my jaw drop open. Does she think we're playing Monopoly?

"Where on earth would I find the extra two grand?" I whisper harshly.

"Not a problem," she retorts breezily. "We can bargain them down. Come on, Mum, let's go and see it."

There's that winning expression she's so good at. I feel myself weakening.

"All right, we'll take a look," I say resignedly. "But first I must use a toilet."

The agent graciously allows me to use the tiny loo off a corner of his office, practically filled with cleaning materials but still affording relief.

His battered Renault is in sharp contrast to his smart appearance. It's in a long row of dented vehicles, all parked bumper to bumper. I watch amazed as he slowly and purposely drives into the car in front of him. I've hardly recovered from this jolt when he reverses into the one behind in order to get out of a space little bigger than his car. Passers-by seem not to notice this brutal manoeuvre. Perhaps it's a normal part of Parisian life.

During the short trip I wonder suspiciously if his instant availability and eagerness indicate that we're his first potential clients for weeks or whether he's seizing an opportunity to have an English girlfriend – or worse, perhaps he's seen a chance to offload an undesirable residence onto unsuspecting foreigners.

This, my first journey by car in Paris, looks set to be my last as we speed off, narrowly escaping contact with a motorbike emerging suddenly from a side street, then screeching shudderingly to a halt to avoid collision with an oncoming van. Our suave, cool-talking agent winds down his window; he's become a bellowing, wildly gesticulating demon. And the other driver seems to be mirroring him to perfection.

This feels like a nightmare, with traffic building up behind us, the air filled with the dissonance of a thousand French horns. I clutch the sides of my seat, praying I can make it to the next toilet…

I'm already imagining I can see horns of a different kind sprouting through our driver's frizzy black hair when he stops shouting, winds up his window and lets the clutch out suddenly, muttering fiercely to himself. I'm trembling all over as we turn off sharply into a dark, narrow street lined with tall, ancient buildings.

"*Voilà*!" he exclaims, reverting once more to his professional self and bumping the car in front of him as he parks.

I get out shakily, welcoming the solid, unmoving firmness of a pavement beneath my feet.

The agent types a code into a keypad on the wall. He pushes open the heavy wooden door, revealing a dark passage ahead. He presses a glowing button on the crumbling plaster, dimly illuminating a shabby entrance with an uneven, worn wooden staircase spiraling endlessly upwards. We follow him up four flights before I pause, panting for breath.

"Don't these places have lifts?"

The agent turns and smirks, saying something to Nikki.

"He says for the price of this place you can't expect that sort of luxury."

He obviously understands more English than he lets on. I'm beginning to dislike this man. I mentally erase him from my list of prospective sons-in-law.

We plod on, ever upwards.

Arriving at the sixth floor, he produces a large set of keys with a flourish and proceeds to unlock what appears to be the door to a fortress.

"Why so many locks?" I ask Nikki.

"Insurance," she explains. "It's obligatory here to have three locks or they won't cover you."

Following them along a narrow hallway into a fair-sized room, I'm not sure that there's anything worth insuring. Apart from an old-fashioned, grubby sink unit (*stink*-unit, more like) in one corner and a probably unsafe, grease-encrusted gas-cooker in another, there's nothing here. And the previous occupants' colour scheme leaves me cold, with one wall painted black and the other three the deepest possible shade of red. A dim light comes through the large window, which looks onto dingy buildings opposite and fails to block out the constant hum of traffic. Vibration beneath my feet tells me that a Métro line runs directly below the building.

"*Parquet*!" the agent declares suddenly with a distinct note of pride and gabbles rapidly at Nikki.

She translates. “The French value this sort of flooring. It’s an excellent selling point.”

Staring at them, I fail to see anything special about these old wooden floorboards. Obviously, “parquet” means something completely different to the French.

We move towards a much smaller room – the bedroom, I suppose. I’m decidedly unimpressed by the lack of a door, but at least the walls are white.

“Look, Mum, it’s got a bath!” yells Nikki, who has wandered into a room to our left. I throw the agent a quick, embarrassed smile and peep into a space that scarcely allows for standing room. It contains the tiniest bath I’ve ever seen, plus a toilet and sink, which, together with the cracked tiles, must surely harbour the equivalent in germs to the population of Birmingham.

The agent is talking animatedly.

“Apparently, not many Parisian apartments have baths,” Nikki tells me, before my look of disgust wipes out her delight. “You don’t like it, do you?”

“No, Nikki, I don’t. I hate to disappoint you but it’s far too cramped. And I don’t want a place where one of us would be forced to sleep in the kitchen and go through the other’s room to reach that cubbyhole they call a bathroom.”

Hearing the finality of my tone and sensing I’ve lost interest, the agent quickly ushers us out.

Down in the street once more, he shakes our hands with polite formality and hurries off to his car without so much as the offer of a ride back. Making our way to the Métro, I can’t say I’m disappointed.

To add to my worsening mood, it's rush hour. I find myself crushed among hundreds, if not thousands, of travellers whose sole intent seems to be to squeeze into an already over-packed train.

"Watch out for pickpockets!" Nikki whispers urgently from somewhere in this sardine tin.

Is she having a laugh? With my arms pinned firmly to my sides there's absolutely no chance of a stray hand finding its way into my pockets. And anyway, right now my priority is not my worldly goods but the mounting claustrophobia that's making it hard for me to breathe. I feel like I'm going to faint. But even if I do it will go unnoticed since falling in any direction is impossible, hemmed in as I am by my fellow passengers.

Suddenly, to my right, I spy an unoccupied seat right next to the window. Perhaps it's vacant because someone's been sick or peed on it. Regardless, I set my sights on it. I need to sit down.

"*Pardon*!" I say loudly several times, pushing my way past human obstacles to reach it, tripping over the feet of a large woman sitting beside the space. Her body language conveys clearly her unwillingness to move across to make room for me. She heaves a heavy sigh as I fall onto the seat next to her, relieved to find it unsoiled.

I've often noticed on Parisian buses and trains that people select the position nearest the aisle, seeming to dare anyone to push past them to sit on the window seat. There may be several such places yet passengers will remain squashed uncomfortably together rather than try to reach one. But for the moment I neither know nor care why that is.

Fortunately *Nation*, being a major Métro interchange where many folk get off, is also our destination. I'm propelled forward with the throng, reaching the platform just before the doors close.

Nikki miraculously materialises from the crowd and we walk through a maze of passages that echo with sounds of a busker playing an accordion, the cries of a fruit and vegetable stallholder urging us to take advantage of his special offers and the ceaseless clatter and chatter of feet and voices.

We find our way out of this surreal subterranean world and reach the bustle of Parisian street life, a place of confusion, to me at least, where many roads converge on a massive roundabout. Watching traffic moving apparently randomly in all directions with no lane markings, I can't help but stand and watch in awe at the seemingly disorganized interweaving of cars, motorbikes and even bicycles. There must surely be some rules underlying this chaos though I've no idea what they are.

"Come on Mum, we've got to cross the road here. Follow me. I know what I'm doing." I wish I shared her confidence.

As we step onto what looks like a pedestrian crossing I'm horrified to see a car heading straight towards us with no apparent intention of stopping. I freeze. Nikki pulls my arm.

"Don't stop now Mum. You'll be ok. It's an offence to kill a pedestrian in Paris."

Somehow we make it to the other side of the road unscathed, though I'm left trying to figure out how we did it.

Back at last in the apartment, I'm so glad the day is nearing its close that even the cat leaping onto my lap, gripping my skirt with its claws, raising its tail and pointing its backside at my face, fails to generate the usual annoyance.

"Tomorrow, the weekly property paper comes out. We'll get up early and start hunting in earnest," Nikki calls from the kitchen.

Luckily, she can't see my reaction.

*

It's 9.30a.m. We've already breakfasted in true Continental style on coffee and freshly baked croissants from a local bakery and are studying the weekly property news.

"This sounds good value," Nikki announces. "It's in the 18th *arrondissement* and at sixty thousand Euros is well with our budget, with money to spare for furnishings."

Our budget? Is she proposing to contribute her overdraft? I keep my thoughts to myself…

"What's an *arrondissement*?" I ask.

"Paris is divided into twenty districts," she explains, "each one with a number. The 18th is particularly popular. Most of it's called *Montmartre*. It's where the *Moulin Rouge* is."

"Isn't that the Red Light district?" I ask suspiciously.

"Well, yes, but that's only a part of it. It's very cosmopolitan, lots going on, there's the artists' quarter and the *Sacré-Coeur*. It would be a great place to live."

"So what's the catch?"

"It says *travaux à faire.*"

"Work to do?" I translate. "What sort of work?"

"Well… a bit of doing up, I should think. You know, surface stuff, like decorating."

My mind flits through various alternative possibilities – Leaking gas? Rotting window frames? Unsafe electrics? Cracks in the brickwork…?

Nikki, meanwhile, is dialling a number on her mobile. She speaks rapidly to someone, then turns to me.

"I've spoken to the owner. He says the apartment is empty and he'll meet us at *Barbès-Rochechouart* Métro station in an hour. I've told him to look out for a short English woman."

"I'm not that small," I protest.

"No, I meant me."

I have to remind myself that for all her diminutive build, she's a fully-grown, capable woman and no longer my little girl.

As we set off, I'm hoping that this time we'll find a real bargain. At least we've missed the busy period so we both find seats on the train. In less than half an hour we're standing outside the almost unpronounceable *Barbès-Rochechouart* station. The sun is shining on a busy Parisian boulevard. And with all the liveliness that characterizes this vibrant city, this promises to be a much pleasanter experience than yesterday.

A tall, grey-haired man approaches us.

"*Bonjour. La Petite Anglaise*?" He beams at

Nikki, shakes her hand and accords me the same courtesy.

Listening to him and Nikki chatting animatedly in French, it's hard to believe they've only just met. How on earth can they find so much to talk about after only a few seconds' acquaintance?

I follow them under the vast iron bridge that carries the Métro overhead, across a wide, busy road – another game of Dodge-The-Homicidal-Driver – and we turn off into a dark side street that gives a distinct impression of seediness. Even the sun has disappeared quickly behind a cloud.

However, my mood lightens instantly when an ornately carved door opens onto a spacious foyer with a colourful splash of plants and a piano against one wall. The sight of such an unexpected item in the entrance is soon explained when Nikki, who can't resist showing off her musical talent, begins to perform. Half the notes don't play while the rest are excruciatingly out of tune. The instrument's probably awaiting disposal. And if she continues to make this noise, we'll be going with it.

I glance around hoping to see a lift. But no – it's a trudge up several flights to the top floor. Some of the last few stairs are piled high with boxes of books, clothes, shoes and bric-a-brac. Obviously someone's moving out.

The owner's smile as he opens a door fails to soften the blow as we are confronted with a narrow, foul-smelling hallway littered with unidentifiable debris. I catch sight of a stained, seatless toilet.
There's no bathroom or kitchen, just a dowdy room barely big enough to accommodate a bed and a

walk-in area that presumably could be made into a kitchen. Even Nikki doesn't look impressed. She has a brief conversation with the owner.

"There's gas, electricity and running water," she translates.

One look at the ceiling tells me where the water's been running and the damp patch on the floor confirms it. *Travaux à faire*? I reflect cynically. It would take a lot more than a few thousand to make this place habitable, even it if were big enough. And you can't build an extension onto a top floor apartment. This place is a complete disaster. Nikki's face tells me she feels the same way.

Buying an apartment in Paris is beginning to lose its appeal.

Chapter *Deux*

With only a week left in Paris, I feel sorely tempted to abandon our now daily nine-to-five apartment-hunt. I'm strongly inclined to resume the normal tourist activities – to gaze at endless works of art in the *Louvre*, breathe in the panoramic view of the city from the steps of the *Sacré-Coeur* and marvel at the traffic failing to have the seemingly-inevitable accidents as each driver negotiates a way towards one of the dozen or so exits radiating off the *Arc de Triomphe*.

However, Nikki, with her ability to focus on and achieve any goal she sets, spurs me on relentlessly, encouraging, coaxing, cajoling me in and out of a dizzying assortment of apartments. Fortunately, we have each bought a *Carte Orange*. This card, used in conjunction with a passport-sized photo, enables us to travel the length and breadth of Paris for a week for the price of an evening meal. The more you use it, the better its value. A few more journeys and we'll have broken even. After that it will feel like we're travelling free.

This week's property guide has become our Bible, with Nikki working her way religiously down the columns of two-roomed apartments. Some of the ones we've looked at would have failed to impress even a family of rats. Clearly unlived-in for ages, they smelt musty and looked as distinctly uncared-for as the buildings that housed them. Surely, with huge cracks in the walls, broken stairs and the stench of household waste, they must be heading towards a Demolition Order. The rest were in striking contrast, with large, tastefully decorated rooms, glorious views and carpeted stairs leading up to them. Their sole drawback was the price, which Nikki dismissed lightly as "only a few more thousand pounds, Mum…" whilst I took a decidedly more realistic view, trying to impress on her that at our time of life her dad and I cannot afford to take on a second mortgage.

None of the estate agents who showed us around admitted to speaking English. Before I came to Paris, I thought everyone here spoke English. I was under the impression that only we British were poor linguists.

*

8.00am.

I'm buttering baguettes while Nikki scans this week's copy of the property newspaper. Its pages have scarcely touched the coffee table's surface before she calls me over. Reluctant to dampen her enthusiasm with the cold water of my pessimistic outlook, I peer over her shoulder. The only bit I really understand in the short paragraph she's pointing to is the price: fifty-nine thousand Euros, just under forty thousand pounds.

"It's a private ad for a small apartment on the outskirts of Paris, *deux pieces* – that's two rooms - completely refurbished, not overlooked, parquet flooring and low charges. And what's more, the price is right," Nikki reels off in one breath.

Yes, for 'small' read 'cramped', 'not overlooked' indicates 'tower block', 'refurbished', it's barely habitable and as for 'parquet' – well, that's just floorboards. And the charges are 'minimal' for someone who's well off, I think sceptically.

"Sounds ok so far," I say out loud.

Undeterred by my non-committal response, Nikki is already dialling the number. A brief conversation and she's on her feet.

"We'll have to hurry, Mum. He's got someone else going to look at it. But we'll be first if we meet him there in an hour's time."

Oh, yeah. Isn't there always someone else who's interested?

I keep my cynicism to myself as I rush through breakfast, grab my jacket and follow Nikki down four flights of stairs – as usual, the lift is out of order.

We've overestimated the length of the journey. Six Métro stops and a five-minute bus ride find us studying the unremarkable façade of a stone-clad five-storey building with a couple of shops on either side of a heavy, panelled oak door.

"We've still got half an hour to spare, Mum. How about we find out about the neighbours?"

"What do you mean?" I asks suspiciously knowing how outrageous Nikki can be at times, striking up intimate conversations with perfect strangers. "You're not thinking of knocking on people's doors, are you?"

"No, nothing like that. Let's get a feel for what the place is like, shall we?"

Without waiting for a reply, she disappears into a grocer's shop, whilst I remain outside trying to look interested in a box of potatoes.

Ten minutes later she emerges, smiling.

"He says this is a really friendly area. So that's a good start, isn't it?"

He took ten minutes to say that?

"Nikki, wait," I call as she heads for a nearby bar. But she disappears inside. This time I follow her and stand grinning uncomfortably, trying to look as if I'm there for a purpose as she chats up the barman.

"I need a toilet," I whisper in Nikki's ear.

Somehow she manages to integrate this into her next sentence.

The barman points to the back door with a theatrical flourish announcing loudly, "*La toilette, Madame!*"

Flushed with embarrassment, I weave my way through the all-male clientele and dense cigarette smoke into a small yard, where an ancient sign saying "*TOILETTE*" hangs lopsidedly from a rusty nail on a loosely fitting wooden door.

"This seems like a nice part of Paris," Nikki decides as we risk life and limb once more to cross the road.

We dodge out of the path of a silver Citroen cruising along the pavement and, flattened against the door to the apartments, I watch dumbfounded as the driver, still ignoring the road, pulls to a halt, gets out, locks the car and walks towards us.

"Madame Fielding?" he queries. I nod automatically.

He smiles, extending a hand. "Henri Dupont."

I return the gesture, aware that my hand is not

the only body part shaking, whilst Nikki, who doesn't seem the slightest bit fazed, launches into what sounds like a quick-fire question and answer session. She frowns as a young couple approach.

"He's thinking of letting it if he doesn't sell quickly," she informs me. "And he says these people have come to look at the apartment with a view to renting it. So he's showing them round first."

"Nikki, let's not bother then…" I begin.

"Oh, Mum, now we've come this far, we might as well give it the once over," she pleads.

Who am I to argue with such impeccable logic?

The couple disappear inside with Monsieur Dupont, leaving me feeling disgruntled that, not content with trying to run us over, he now seems to be regarding us as runners-up in the race to look round the apartment. Perhaps he thinks the English don't mind queuing.

I'm on the verge of telling Nikki that we've waited long enough when they all reappear amid smiles and handshakes.

Monsieur Dupont nods at us, holding the door wide for us to enter, his mouth curling downwards at the corners. I suspect it's meant to be a smile.

The moment he speaks, Nikki falls easily into her role as interpreter. "He says this is the entrance."

Does he, indeed? He must have already decided we're a couple of idiots. What else could this large space, with wall-mounted post-boxes to our right and stairs straight ahead, possibly be?

"And to the left of the stairs a door leads down

to the cellar," Nikki continues.

I fantasise about endless racks filled with fine French wines, whilst Monsieur Dupont inserts a key to open the door, except in this case it doesn't.

He mumbles something to himself, then rattles off a few words to Nikki.

"He says he's brought the wrong key. He never goes down there."

Well, who wants to see a gloomy cellar anyway?

Three flights up the narrow staircase he turns sharply to the right and unlocks a door, whilst continuing to converse with Nikki.

"From the next landing you get an excellent view of the Eiffel Tower," she says excitedly, as we step into a white-painted hallway.

To our right is what must be the kitchen. At any rate, it's a room with a sink. Sunshine is streaming through the window, reflecting off its white walls. Its odd shape reminds me of that bit of jigsaw that doesn't seem to fit anywhere. How on earth you could get a square cooker, let alone a fridge/freezer, into this tiny space requires the sort of mental gymnastics I'll deal with if I have to.

Further along on the right a 'deceptively small' room contains a sink, a miniscule shower cubicle with no curtain and a toilet beside the window. Very basic, but with sunlight brightening its white walls I rather warm to the idea of viewing Paris while I'm sitting on the loo. However, it's overlooked to one side and if I can see out, others can see in.

At the end of the hallway is a larger room,

again painted white. Either it's his favourite colour or white paint is on special offer.

We walk to the far side of the room, roughly three strides, to gaze in awe at the rooftops of Paris.

"All the windows are double glazed," Nikki informs me.

The last room, overlooking the front street, is as bright and compact as the others. I'm getting a really good feeling. Nikki looks equally impressed. I think I'm sold on this place. And perhaps it's sold to me. The basic layout is just what I had in mind.

"This could be my bedroom," Nikki whispers. From her expression I can see that she's already mentally decorating the larger of the two rooms. For my part I'm reluctant to appear too eager and rule out any chance of bargaining over the price.

Too late! Nikki's enthusiasm is hardly in doubt as she beams at the owner and nods happily as they chat. For all I know she's already told him we'll buy it.

"Nikki, ask him if he'll drop the price a bit. Offer him two thousand pounds less – or the equivalent in Euros."

The sudden tautening of his mouth beneath the little moustache and a furrow appearing between his bushy eyebrows convey his response even before Nikki begins to translate.

"No, that's the lowest he'll go," she tells me.

I try to deal with the disappointment at being denied an opportunity to bargain.

"Apparently, it's a very fair price for this part of Paris and if we buy directly through his newspaper advert we avoid paying estate agents' fees."

"No, Nikki, *he* has to pay those," I argue.

After a further discussion with Monsieur Dupont, Nikki explains that things work differently in France, a conclusion I'm rapidly reaching for myself.

"It's the buyer who pays for the estate agent and the solicitor for both parties," she informs me.

"So we save on the agent but how much will we have to pay for the solicitor?"

Another brief, rapid-fire conversation.

"He says it's not a large amount. Otherwise, how would first-time buyers be able to afford a place of their own?"

"Right, we'll take it," I say casually, as if I were buying an elegant suit from Marks & Spencer's.

Several smiles, handshakes and exchanges of phone numbers later, I find myself walking briskly down the hill beside Nikki. I cannot believe I've actually agreed to buy an apartment in Paris. I'm shocked, stunned by the ease with which I'm spending our hard-earned money without the shred of an idea about how to tackle the whole affair.

Nikki appears deep in thought as we munch our way through salad-filled baguettes and share a carafe of red wine in a bar near the Métro.

After a couple of glasses I'm still shell-shocked, still trying to grapple with the enormity of what I've just done. It feels like I'm acting in a play with no script.

The ringtone of Nikki's mobile makes us both jump.

"Ah, Monsieur Dupont!" she exclaims.

He seems to be doing most of the talking, with Nikki doing an excellent impression of a nodding dog and repeating "*Oui*" and "*D'accord*", using a vast range of inflections.

"*A bientôt,*" she concludes, putting her phone back on the table.

"What's happening soon?" I ask.

"Monsieur Dupont says he's made an appointment with his solicitor and he'll take us there by car. He says it's best if we buy *sous la table*, which means "under the table."

Is it the effect of the wine, or are events spinning rapidly out of control?

I take a deep breath. "Nikki, I know you're talking English but I don't understand anything you've said. Can you repeat everything – slowly, and very, very simply?"

"Ok, sorry, Mum. I should have explained what he told me. When you agree to buy a property in France, you sign a *promesse de vente* in the presence of a solicitor. This "promise of sale" is legally binding and you pay ten percent of the agreed price, which you lose if you withdraw from the sale. Then in three months time, when all the legal paperwork is complete, there's a final signing. Monsieur Dupont said it would benefit both parties if you pay him eight thousand Euros in cash under the table and officially declare the sale price as fifty-one thousand. Then he'll pay less tax on the sale and you'll be charged a lower owner's tax each year. I think I've got the facts right."

"I still don't understand the bit about 'under the

table'. What table?"

"I'm not sure. I think it's a sort of tradition. I'll ask my friend's mum about it. She owns an apartment."

I'm more confused than ever but remain silent, not wanting to lose the plot completely…

"He's made an appointment for the day after tomorrow and he'll pick us up at one o'clock outside the apartment."

"Which apartment?"

"The new one, of course"

I'm struggling to digest all this.

"Nikki, how am I going to get thousands of pounds as a down payment in two days?"

"Oh, Dad will know the answer to that," she says breezily.

I'm not sure I share her optimism but I ring Dennis, who seems pleased we've got this far and says he'll phone his bank about transferring money and get back to us.

A short while later my mobile rings. I don't bother to tell Dennis he's caught me on the toilet again. At least this one has a seat, which I've carefully lined with toilet paper from the wadge I've got used to carrying in my pocket at all times. You can't be too careful…

"Right, it's sorted," he says. "My bank can transfer money to a French account in twenty-four hours"

"But I don't have a French bank account," I protest.

"Ask Nikki if we can put it in hers. And good luck."

We're certainly going to need plenty of that, I reflect, trying to flush away half a toilet roll.

Nikki phones Dennis with her bank details and we visit her bank to see her financial assistant, whose expression changes from wariness to interest as Nikki informs her of the imminent arrival of six thousand Euros. It seems that in the space of a few minutes, Nikki has become a valued customer. They chatter on for several minutes more than I'd have thought necessary, too fast for me to understand.

"What was all that about?" I ask as we leave the bank.

"Oh, she was simply suggesting ways for me to invest my money."

Little does the assistant realise that in a few days Nikki's apparent windfall will disappear. Most of it is our ten percent deposit.

At long last we have time to relax, perhaps to stroll along the tree-lined *Champs-Elysées* or sit peacefully beside the Seine…

"Mum," Nikki interrupts, "let's go to the *Mairie* – that's the Town Hall – and check there are no plans to knock down the apartment block to make way for a motorway or anything else in a few years' time."

Her businesslike approach seems too sensible to argue with.

The grand building overlooks a bustling square and is attractively adorned with floral displays. A man at the reception desk directs us to the second floor, where the numerous doors on the long corridor are unmarked. How on earth are we supposed to know which one we want?

Nikki knocks on a door at random. It's opened by a woman who redirects us to the fifth floor, telling us to seek out the fourth door on the right when we get out of the lift…

This room looks more promising. A smartly dressed young man invites us in and Nikki plunges straight into business mode, asking endless questions. He directs our attention to some complicated-looking charts lining the walls. They apparently represent the local development plans. I hope they mean more to Nikki than they do to me.

We leave with smiles and handshakes.

"*Merci,*" I say, determined to make an effort to show my appreciation and some knowledge of the language.

"We're lucky, Mum," Nikki tells me. "Not only are there no future plans to knock down our apartment, but in five years' time there'll be a tramway going right past our place. That will make it worth more when we sell."

So this is now *our* apartment - and Nikki is already planning to sell it even though we haven't yet paid for it. I can't think beyond tomorrow, never mind five years down the tramline.

"Mum, one of my friends' mums would love to meet you. Do you fancy dropping in on her? It's only a couple of Métro stops from here."

I agree, eagerly welcoming this distraction from the bewildering complexities of buying an apartment.

Hélène embraces me like an old friend, kissing me warmly on both cheeks. I don't even know her and we're already on kissing and hugging terms!

She proceeds to enthuse in broken English about the wisdom of buying an apartment locally.

This area is set to become a thriving cultural centre. It's an excellent investment, it would seem, and what's more, buying "under the table" is very common, she assures me. Lots of people do it.

Several glasses of wine later I'm beginning to feel quite optimistic about the future. I even try out my pidgin French, much to Hélène's delight and Nikki's amusement.

The more the drink flows the better my French flows until, by the time we stumble to the Métro and finally arrive at Nikki's friend's place, I'm sure I've made unbelievably vast strides with the language.

Chapter *Trois*

Nikki wakes me early with a mug of strong, black coffee.

"You were in great form last night, Mum. I had no idea you knew so much French."

I try to focus on the previous evening but the thumping in my head blocks out whatever feats of verbal dexterity I may have performed.

"Neither did I," I mumble.

"Well you had us both in stitches anyway."

I decide not to pursue this line of conversation in case I hear something I'd prefer not to know. Like my daughter I can sometimes be outrageous.

We spend the morning trying to assemble the documents and information we need to take to the solicitor's this afternoon.

Passport – got that. My current French address – got that too: I apparently live in an apartment owned by the grandmother of Nikki's friend Sylvie. Sylvie informed us that we need an address in France to avoid complications and assured us that her grandmother won't mind – even if she ever finds out! I don't know whether this is strictly necessary but I'm willing to do anything that makes for a smooth transaction.

Documents like marriage and birth certificates can be sent on later.

Nikki phones her bank to confirm that Dennis' money order has arrived and we set off to meet Monsieur Dupont.

I wince as he shakes my hand a little too firmly and climb into the front of the motorised skip he calls a car (or rather, *une voiture*). Its floor is littered with papers, empty cola cans and objects of uncertain identity. I shuffle my feet around to make a bit of space. Nikki does the same in the back. We are well on our way before I've managed to locate and fit my seat belt.

En route, Nikki alternates between chatting with Monsieur Dupont and translating for me. She informs me that he's a *kinaestherapist* who does various sorts of massage. The way this rickety motor is bouncing along, throwing me forward at every junction, I feel I'm going to be sorely in need of his skills.

We come to an abrupt halt outside a magnificent building somewhere in the suburbs. The door is opened by a smiling, pretty-faced woman whom I presume to be the secretary. She ushers us into a grand room with expensive leather furniture, high ceiling and ornately framed paintings. Even Louis XIV would not have felt out of place entertaining in such opulent surroundings.

"*Bonjour.*"

A tall man, possibly in his mid thirties, rises from behind his huge desk and shakes our hands.

"*Asseyez-vous,*" he says indicating the comfortable-looking chairs.

I begin to feel rather uneasy as I note the discrepancy between the way Nikki and I are dressed compared with Monsieur Dupont and his solicitor (or "*notaire*" as Nikki informed me he's called). The notaire is wearing a tailored, dark-blue suit complete with waistcoat, pristine white shirt and crimson tie; Monsieur Dupont looks immaculate (unlike his car) in a spotless cream suit and shirt with brown tie; whereas Nikki is wearing her red, ill-fitting sweater and those modern jeans with designer rips in them. My own attire is hardly better – faded blue jeans, sandals and light-blue tee shirt. It hadn't even occurred to me that this might be a formal occasion.

However, if the notaire feels any disdain, he keeps it well hidden as he peruses my documentation and explains to Nikki the papers I'll be signing.

Nikki turns to me. "Mum, the notaire says you're welcome to question anything you don't understand."

If I do that, I think, we'll be here for the rest of the week…

"Thanks," I respond weakly.

I sign obediently where I'm directed and Nikki passes across a cheque for ten percent of the "official" price – five thousand, one hundred Euros - with a grand flourish. That's over three and a half thousand pounds gone in an instant.

The notaire stands, a signal that the process has ended.

And that's it. Handshakes all round and we walk out into the sunshine. I reflect on how easy this seems so far – way too easy, in fact. There has to be a catch somewhere…

Monsieur Dupont drops us off in the city and, with one more day before my return to England, Nikki and I decide to spend time at Ikea getting ideas for furnishing the apartment. Then when I return in three months time for the final signing, we'll have a clearer picture of what we need to buy. Ikea is a fair distance outside Paris. Like two hyperactive children we jump onto a train and head out towards the suburbs, where we get off at a quiet, outlying station. It's a good job Nikki's been here before and knows which bus to catch.

I've already learnt that queues mean nothing at bus stops in Paris and we fight our way onto the crowded bus along with everyone else –Ikea must be regarded as a good day out. I've lost sight of Nikki but I know she's somewhere on the bus.

There seems to be no limit to the number of passengers allowed. My feet are being trodden on and I'm being buffeted by bodies all round me, with babies screaming, teenagers shouting into mobile phones and old ladies complaining loudly to each other. Each time the bus stops there's a general surge as people force their way towards the exit and another as more push their way on. This is hell on wheels.

Finally, seeing the huge Ikea sign, I realise we've arrived – but there seems to be a problem. Both doors of the bus are surrounded by stern faced men demanding to see passengers' tickets. Presumably they are ticket inspectors. Do they always hunt in packs, I wonder? I sense the tension round me and there's a long delay while each ticket or pass is studied in detail. However, I'm not worried – we bought tickets in a tobacconist's before our journey.

I approach an inspector confidently, thrusting my ticket under his nose. He frowns at me.

"*Non, non!*" He wags a finger in front of my

face.

What have I done wrong?

"Pardon, je suis Anglaise," I say uncertainly. *"Est-ce qu'il ya un problème?"*

"Can I 'elp you, Madame?" another passenger intervenes. "I can spik a leedle Engleesh."

What a relief!

"What's the matter with my ticket?"

"Is no good unless you put in machine on bus before you travel. Machine prints date on ticket for… for… *valider*…

Light dawns. "You mean I have to validate my ticket by getting a machine to stamp it," I say. I remember doing something like that in Italy. "I didn't realise I had to do it in France."

Other passengers are beginning to grow even more impatient than they already were. My helper says something to the inspector – the only word I recognise is "*Anglaise*". It seems to do the trick.

"Ok, this once," the inspector growls in English. "Next time, machine…" He dismisses me with a wave of his hand.

My legs are shaking. I spot Nikki looking for me and start to tell her what's just happened.

"Don't worry about it, Mum. You'll know what to do next time."

She takes my arm and leads me towards the entrance.

The bus incident and the long, uncomfortable journey have taken their toll.

"Nikki, I need a toilet – urgently."

An escalator takes us up to an enormous area filled with a colourful display of chairs, cushions and throws. People are milling everywhere. But for the moment I'm interested in only one thing. Giant coloured footprints indicate directions to various parts of the store, but I can't see a sign saying *toilettes*. And I'm desperate.

"Mum, feel how soft this is." Nikki is already absorbed in the soft furnishings.

"Nikki, this is an emergency," I say tersely. "If I don't go now, it'll be soft *and* wet."

One look at my face and she changes her attention to searching for a toilet.

Ah, an assistant!

"Ou est la toilette?" I ask.

Nikki translates the reply. "She says she doesn't work in this department."

We accost another assistant who is passing. I repeat the question.

"She's sorry, she only works at a checkout," Nikki says.

I'm on the point of leaking when I notice a sign pointing down a flight of stairs indicating *Toilettes.*

I don't think I've ever been so relieved.

At the bottom of the stairs I reach my destination. Heaven couldn't offer anything better than this!

On the way out I notice a couple of men urinating but fortunately, they're too intent on what they're doing to notice me. In my hurry to get in, I hadn't noticed the urinals or the symbol on the door…

Nikki is not outside the loo. In fact she's nowhere to be seen. And finding one's way round this vast emporium seems to involve a logic I don't possess. I'm utterly lost.

She isn't in the brightly coloured toy department, the artificial flower section, the lighting area…

Eventually I find her trying out beds for comfort.

"This one's brilliant!" she calls to me, bouncing on a fully made double bed, completely unaware that I've been searching for her.

I flop onto a bed beside her, grateful for a few minutes' respite. People passing look at us as though we're some kind of freaks. Don't the French test beds? After all, we spend a third of our lives in them.

I can see where Nikki's been by the trail of ruffled bedclothes. I hurriedly suggest we go and eat.

After a quick snack in the store's restaurant, we wander through the endless maze that is Ikea. I sink into a leather sofa, while Nikki admires elegantly laid family-sized tables that wouldn't even go up the stairwell, let alone through the door of the apartment.

She throws herself onto a sofa bed.

"This would look lovely in my bedsit…"

Oh, so her bedroom has now developed into self-contained quarters.

"Nikki, we must be practical," I say firmly. "The flat is thirty square metres altogether, not a hundred and thirty, so everything will have to be as compact as possible – and don't forget there's the narrow, twisty staircase to be negotiated. Most of this stuff wouldn't even go up there."

It feels like we're equipping a doll's house. Maybe we should be visiting a toyshop instead…

I discover a narrow, white, folding melamine table with drawers at each end and flaps that extend outwards. Perfect!

But when I look round to show Nikki, she's disappeared again.

I finally catch up with her in the bathroom area where she's closely examining a shower curtain covered with blisters of various coloured liquids.

"Mum, this would be ideal to brighten up the shower room."

"Er, yes, it's quite attractive," I say, beginning to feel somewhat frustrated that our priorities for furnishing the apartment are so far apart.

Suddenly I catch sight of just what I want for my room – a mezzanine, a double bed in the air accessed by a ladder, leaving plenty of space beneath for other furniture. They're specially designed for small apartments. I'm not sure that Dennis will enjoy sleeping near the ceiling, but what the heck, he's not here and the choice is mine…

At this point I wish we'd made a list. We're choosing things haphazardly but Nikki's confident we'll remember everything when I return in September.

Both of us are exhausted but happy with what we've seen. We leave Ikea empty-handed but with an enormous mental list of items we'll probably have forgotten by tomorrow. And I'm aware that we haven't yet found a cooker, fridge or freezer. Oh, well, never mind…

We enjoy a happy evening at the cinema watching a romantic movie and end the day with a Chinese takeaway and a bottle of wine.

Chapter *Quatre*

It doesn't feel like three months since I was last in Paris.

I'm pleased to be back. I love what I've already experienced of the language, the multicultured lifestyle, the food, the so un-English way of life. Everything about this wonderful city is fascinatingly different, even if occasionally frustrating.

Nikki and I are staying in Sylvie's grandma's apartment (a woman I've never actually met).

Nikki's current boyfriend Marcel has offered to check out my prospective purchase.

"Does he work for a building firm?" I enquire.

"No, he's a computer analyst. But he's lived in a lot of apartments so he'll know if ours is sound."

Rather late, I think, since in two days I'm signing the final papers and would lose my large deposit if I withdrew now. However, not wanting to seem churlish I agree and Nikki arranges another visit to the apartment.

Marcel walks slowly round each room, wearing a thoughtful expression, knocking on walls as he goes. Finally he smiles at me, nods vigorously and declares, "*Oui, c'est bon!*"

Is that it? Perhaps he has a gift for wall-knocking, equivalent to water-divining, revealing unseen things the rest of us can't discover with our obviously limited perceptions. I must admit I had hoped for a more scientific assessment.

But hiding my disappointment I treat the three of us to lunch in celebration of Marcel's knocking skills. I hope his computing abilities are more evident if he's going to end up supporting my daughter.

I pass the evening arranging and rearranging the pile of documentation to take with me tomorrow to create a semblance of being organised. I've got birth certificates for Dennis, the children and myself, our marriage certificate, my passport…

There are various other papers connected with the purchase that are part of the package but I've no idea what they're about. They arrived by post so I've brought them with me.

*

Today feels second in importance only to our wedding day – but this time it feels like I'm on my own. I know Dennis can't help being a home bird but I wish he were with me right now. However, he's expressed the utmost confidence in being able to leave the whole affair to me though, of course, he'll happily enjoy the fruits of my labours and our joint savings!

I explained to him what the notaire said - that, under French law, unless we sign *en tontine* – a special arrangement for couples buying property – upon my demise, the children will be the sole inheritors of our apartment. But being a generous soul, he's not troubled by such trivialities.

This time Nikki and I are preparing properly for the ceremonious occasion and we're juggling for space in the tiny bathroom to wash and carefully apply makeup. Yesterday we even fitted in hair appointments.

I choose a navy blue suit with red blouse and matching shoes whilst Nikki opts for a purple dress that flatters her figure and silver slingback sandals. Both drenched in expensive perfume, we set off with ample time to meet Nikki's English-speaking friend Annette, who's taking us by car to the notaire's office and will ensure that today's procedure goes to plan. Since she's recently bought a property of her own we were happy to accept her kind offer. And she'll certainly know more than we do, which is nothing.

I should have used the toilet before we left as my nerves have travelled to my bladder. Being in Parisian traffic invariably pushes me to the verge of incontinence. By the time we arrive I'm fit to burst.

I urgently ask the secretary for the toilet, noting with satisfaction how confidently I make this request in French.

My needs dealt with, I emerge relieved. The secretary shows me into the notaire's plush office where Nikki, Annette and Monsieur Dupont have already gathered.

"*Bonjour.*" The notaire greets each of us with a strong handshake that gives me the feeling that he's firmly in control of the situation. I'm glad someone is!

Despite our finery I'm beginning to sense that Nikki and I are horribly out of place. We hadn't realised that not only is this a formal occasion but it's also a solemn one. The atmosphere in the room is heavily sombre, almost funereal. The three French people are clothed from head to foot in black.

We're all standing straight-backed in deadly silence. The notaire has taken on the demeanour of a clergyman. Are we shortly to be asked to kneel or join our hands in prayer, I wonder wildly.

I shoot a glance of panic in Nikki's direction. She looks distinctly unconcerned. Perhaps living in France she's learnt to expect the unexpected.

With one movement of the notaire's hand we obediently sit, hands folded, watching him watching us. He says something to me in French, which sounds polite in tone though the only word I understand is *vous.*

I must look as bewildered as I feel, since Annette whispers to me, "He's asking for your documentation."

I hand over my package and we wait as he peruses each item in turn. I feel very ill at ease with this seemingly interminable silence. Couldn't we have sat and chatted or gone out for a coffee while he spent the best part of half an hour on this task?

Suddenly the notaire picks up an enormous wadge of papers, stands, clears his throat and begins to read out loud. For all the world he could be quoting from Macbeth. The words coming out of his mouth are pronounced slowly, clearly and extremely dramatically. I'm seized with an almost uncontrollable urge to laugh as the speech unfolds, steadily increasing in intensity, presumably for maximum effect. Has he been to drama school? Every so often there's a significant pause, which I'm convinced means he's either coming to an end or waiting for around of applause. But no – on and on he drones and I haven't a clue what he's talking about.

Stifling my giggles, knowing how dreadfully embarrassed I'd feel if he stopped mid-flow and everyone stared at me, I distract myself with the ornately-framed paintings, the décor, the blue velvet curtains – anything...

At last the notaire sits. I breathe an inaudible sigh of relief. I've just sat through the longest hour-and-a-half of my life. It's impossible to discern what the others are feeling.

The notaire rises again, walks round his desk to Mr Dupont, whispers in his ear, looks meaningfully at the rest of us and abruptly leaves the room.

Annette leans across. "It's *sous-la-table* time," she whispers to me. "The notaire is not supposed to know or see what you are about to do, so he is leaving the room for a short while to give you time."

"Ah, I see. He doesn't witness it so it can't have happened. Is that it?"

"Absolument!"

From my bag I remove the large, bulky envelope containing eight thousand Euros in cash and pass it beneath the table towards Monsieur Dupont, who simultaneously reaches across the top of the table. Blushing with embarrassment I realise that *sous-la-table* does not literally mean "under the table" – it's merely a figure of speech.

I watch anxiously as he counts the money with a speed that suggests he's done this before. He nods at me, smiles smugly and puts it in his briefcase. We wait a further five silent minutes for the notaire to return.

He re-enters the room, his face impassive, sits behind his desk and looks directly at me. "The cheque, Madame?" he requests, in a passably English accent. Belatedly, I recall that Monsieur Dupont told me that this notaire speaks English and hurriedly sift through my memory to see whether I've said anything since we arrived that he shouldn't have heard.

Nikki passes her cheque to me and I hand it across to the notaire, who studies it intently.

He stands, nods at Monsieur Dupont, who gives me two sets of keys and there are handshakes and smiles all round.

"Have I really just bought a French apartment?" I whisper to Annette on the way out, clutching the massive folder of documentation the notaire placed in my hands.

"Yes," she says. "It's completely legal now. You can move in as soon as you like."

.Chapter *Cinq*

It's seven thirty and we're up, dressed and in high spirits as we bite into soft, warm flaky pastries with bits of chocolate inside, freshly made this morning in the nearby patisserie. *Pains au chocolat* are Nikki's favourite. And the French have a right to be proud of their coffee. This is what I call breakfast – so much better than a bowl of soggy cornflakes!

We park our bags of belongings inside the door of the grandma's apartment, to be picked up later by Marcel – Nikki has lent him the key. We make sure everything's clean and tidy, lock up and walk to the Métro.

Unfortunately, the rest of Paris seems to be doing the same and my mood is plummeting by the second as I fail to reach the only visible free seat at the end of the carriage.

Luckily, the bus is less crowded. As soon as it moves off someone presses a red button on one of the handrails and a red display, *ARRET DEMANDE,* lights up close to the ceiling at the front of the bus. Nikki explains that this alerts the driver to the fact that someone wants to get off at the next stop. I file this away for future reference.

I look at my fellow passengers. It's as though we've stepped into the heart of Africa. Apart from the two of us, everyone else is black and dressed in gloriously bright, flowing, colourful robes, including the men. Nikki had told me that many of the suburbs of Paris were particularly multicultural but I hadn't understood to what extent this was so.

Nikki's mobile rings. She speaks briefly in French, ends the call and turns to me.

"Mum, you know I'm on the books of a temping agency for a computer firm? Well, they've asked me to do a week's work and they want me there today. I'm terribly sorry to leave you on your own but I daren't turn them down. My bank's already threatened to close my account."

"Don't worry, darling," I say light-heartedly, feeling panic welling up inside. "I'll be fine. It'll be a good chance for me to practise my French and not rely on you."

She looks grateful.

We get off the bus and cross the road. I tap the code into the keypad on the wall and open the door. Nikki apologises non-stop all the way up to the apartment. Its whitewashed walls gleam brightly in the sunshine. Nikki pulls down the lever in the kitchen that turns on the water at the mains. She's already arranged for someone from EDF to come and switch on the gas and electricity.

"He'll be here shortly, Mum," she says, hugging me tightly. "But I've got to go now. I'm so sorry. This couldn't have happened at a worse time. I won't be much use to you this week. Are you sure you'll manage?"

"Yes," I say, forcing myself to sound in control.

But I want her to stay, not leave me alone to handle everything. I don't even know where to start. I've got a week to get things up and working and the apartment furnished, ready for Dennis, in an unfamiliar place in a foreign country. Does she think I'm Supermum?

Nikki kisses me on both cheeks – how French she's become! – and I listen to her footsteps going down the stairs. Now I'm alone. A wave of depression sweeps over me.

What on earth have I done? How am I going to make this totally empty apartment, without even a toilet-roll holder, look and feel habitable in just a few days? And worse still, I can't make a cup of tea with no electricity, no kettle, no cup – and no tea.

To make myself feel slightly better I open the shutters and let in the sunshine. Then I decide to do something familiar – use the toilet.

Either I've put on weight or this seat has reached the end of its natural life. A big crack forms in the plastic the moment I sit on it. I remove the broken pieces and crouch over the rim, unsure what germs may be lurking from previous users.

I flush the toilet and wash my hands in the large sink. As I shake them dry (since there's no towel) I notice that the toilet has not stopped flushing. I remove the cistern top and prod at the float. But it makes no difference. And I know the water is metered so that's going to cost me. I go into the kitchen and pull up the red lever to turn off the water. The flushing stops.

I wander aimlessly about the apartment. What are all those wires sticking out of the skirting boards in both rooms? I don't remember seeing them before. What else is wrong with this place? Panic is taking over. My stomach is churning painfully and I need to use the loo again.

I pay closer attention to my surroundings. Looking upwards in the shower-room I notice that the light bulb is hanging by one wire. It's the same in the kitchen. And in the room I've chosen as my bedroom there's not even a bulb, just loose wires.

I can imagine the headlines in the Daily Mail: ENGLISH WOMAN ELECTROCUTED IN PARIS APARTMENT

I feel like crying.

There's a knock on the door. I open it to find God, in the form of a man wearing an EDF badge. At this point I'd be pleased to see anyone.

"*EDF, Madame*," he announces.

I step back into the kitchen doorway to allow him to squeeze past me into the hall. He does something to the electricity meter on the wall and tries a light switch. Well, at least that works.

I move into the hall to give him access to the kitchen. It's like a slow dance, trying to manoeuvre in such a restricted area.

He pulls down a lever high on the wall next to a gas meter, then sniffs suspiciously round a pipe where a cooker would be if we had one.

"*Non, non!*" he exclaims, the only words I understand as he continues with a torrent of French complete with gesticulations. Now he's pushing the lever back up.

"*Parlez-vous anglais?*" I try in desperation.

"*Oui,* a leedle."

"What's the matter? Is there a problem?" I ask, hoping he'll understand better if I speak loudly and very slowly.

"Problem, yes. No gas possible. You 'ave two,

er… *fuites*... er… 'ere, and 'ere." He points to a couple of points on the pipe. "Is *dangereux*."

I can smell gas. He must be telling me it's leaking.

"You need, er… *un plombier*..."

"A plumber?" I ask

"*Oui*, plumber."

I ask him, using what French I can remember and a lot of gestures, if he knows a plumber, because I don't know anyone here. He looks sorry for me and makes a brief call on his mobile.

"Plumber come 'ere t'ree hours."

"*Merci. Merci beaucoup, Monsieur,*" I say gratefully.

I see him out, sit on the floor and burst into floods of tears.

*

I decide to cheer myself up by going out for lunch. I lock up carefully, though I can't think why – I might as well leave the door wide open with a large sign saying 'Help yourself if you can find anything.'

I walk down the stairs and open the door to the street. It's much warmer outside so I don't wait at the bus stop. Striding down the hill I begin to feel more invigorated and ten minutes later I'm ready to take on the world - or at least, the French part of it.

Relaxing in the early autumn sunshine at a table outside a café I order from a smiling waiter, "*Une baguette avec fromage et un café au lait s'il vous plait,*" noting how much better my French is when I'm calm.

And when he brings a cheese baguette and white coffee it's rewarding to know I got it right.

I sip my coffee, observing other customers and passers-by. I so enjoy people watching. Faces convey a great deal of emotion and the French speak almost as much with their hands as with their mouths. Would they feel able to express themselves as effectively without any arm waving? By the time I pay and leave the café I'm in good spirits. But with not quite enough energy to walk back I catch the bus, proud of myself for remembering to activate the *ARRET DEMANDE* sign.

Back in the apartment, instead of focusing on the negative aspects, I plough my energy into visualising the apartment as I'd like it to be, examining each space at length and expanding my powers of imagination until in my mind's eye I've created living quarters that resemble the grandest suite in a top-class hotel…

A loud knock jerks me back to reality. Turning towards the door I notice for the first time a tiny spyhole in the centre. Peering through its fisheye lens I see the distorted face of a man wearing what looks like an official badge.

I open the door partially, leaving the chain on for security, and see a short, smiling, stocky man carrying a toolbox.

"*Bonjour, Madame. EDF. Luigi le plombier à votre service.*"

Luigi? That sounds more Italian than French. And with his Mediterranean complexion he looks

Italian, too.

I unchain the door, let him in and point him towards the kitchen and the faulty pipe. He opens his toolbox and sets to work, singing tunelessly to himself.

Rather than stand over him like an inspector I try to look busy. I really need to pee but since the shower-room door is warped and refuses to close I'll have to wait until the singing plumber leaves. Now, what shall I do?

Perhaps I'll have a go at cleaning the dirty sink in the shower-room, despite the lack of cleaning materials. I pull down the water lever in the kitchen. The toilet cistern immediately starts gurgling.

Trying to ignore it I go into the shower-room, turn on the hot tap and wipe my hand round the basin. Something isn't quite right. For a moment I can't work out what it is. Then I remember that before I went out, I switched on the water heater. Yet the water is stone cold.

Maybe the electricity isn't working. I flick a switch in the hall and the light comes on. A stroke of genius tells me that it must be the water heater that's faulty. Ah well, one more thing wrong with the apartment, then…

I go into Nikki's bedroom-to-be, sit on the floor feeling sorry for myself and grimacing at Luigi's Pavarotti impressions.

The singing stops abruptly. I go into the kitchen, where Luigi proudly displays his soldering. He starts packing up, then stops and turns his head to one side, listening.

He says something in French. I assume he's noticed the noise from the cistern.

"*Parlez-vous anglais?*" I ask hopefully.

"*Non, Madame, français et italien.*" He beams at me.

Luigi seems a friendly sort. Perhaps I can get him to help me if I play the helpless female in distress – I've heard it works with these Continental men.

Taking a deep breath I slowly draw on vocabulary I wasn't aware I knew, words I haven't used since my days as a nanny – they must be still there, somewhere at the back of my head. I manage to explain about the toilet. Suddenly I'm in full flow (verbally, at least!), telling him about everything – the lack of hot water, exposed wires, missing shower rail, dangerous light fittings – touring the apartment with him as I speak and motioning towards each disaster area.

And surprisingly, he understands me.

He fiddles with the cistern and nods knowingly. With a profusion of hand-waving and several false tries, he eventually conveys to me that the flushing mechanism is defunct. I also manage to understand that the electric radiator on the wall next to the toilet has had it as well.

Back in the kitchen he points to the boiler hanging on the wall over the draining board and makes it clear that this, too, is useless.

Despite feeling good about my newly resurrected French I'm on the verge of tears as I contemplate the cost of making this apartment habitable, before I can think about furnishing it.

"But it's going to cost me a fortune, especially *this*," I whine, indicating the boiler. "You're a plumber. How much to do it privately?"

"*Ah, sur le noir!*" he exclaims.

On the black, I translate mentally. That must mean the equivalent of what we call "on the side" – tax-free and cash in hand.

He pauses for a moment, looking at me intently.

"Well, I can get a boiler cheaply," he tells me. "And I'll do the rest of the work for fifty Euros."

"Ok." I've already picked up that this Americanism is universally understood.

"But for the gas pipe I must charge you a hundred and thirty-five Euros because I fixed that on behalf of EDF."

He produces an invoice and I pay him. Luckily I've got plenty of cash handy, since I haven't yet opened a French bank account.

"*Merci, merci*," I say repeatedly as he drains the boiler of water and removes it from the wall.

He doesn't waste much time, I reflect as, puffing fiercely, he staggers out onto the landing with the enormous, enamel-covered cylinder. When he puts it down, it partially blocks the neighbouring door. I hope if someone lives there they won't want to get out in a hurry.

"I'll return with a new boiler in two days," Luigi says, waving two fingers in my face. "And then I'll take this one away. I've got no space in the van today."

I ask for his phone number, which he scribbles on a piece of paper before scurrying off down the stairs.

Looking at the gigantic obstruction he's left, I'm suddenly filled with misgivings.

What if he doesn't come back?

*

I'm staring at the space in the kitchen where the boiler was, half expecting a visit from whoever might live next door. I'm racking my brain, unable to figure out how to explain the offending item on the landing. I can, however, easily imagine a furious, gesticulating, red-faced neighbour bombarding me with a fast-flowing stream of incomprehensible French. Not an ideal first meeting!

An insistent knocking on the door interrupts my ruminating. Fearing the worst, I peep through the spyhole. It's Nikki with an armful of groceries. I can't remember the last time I was so pleased to see her.

"You gave me a fright," I say, opening the door wide. "Why didn't you use the keys I gave you?"

"Sorry, Mum. I forgot I had them." Nikki puts her shopping on the draining board – the only place to put anything that isn't a floor. Smelling something tantalisingly spicy, I realise I'm hungry.

We sit on the floor of the front room to eat the Indian takeaway she's bought. And just as I'm wondering what to eat it with, she produces packets of plastic cutlery. The chicken tikka and pilau rice taste delicious, despite being lukewarm and eaten off bendy paper plates.

"How was your day?" I ask her.

"Tiring. I'm working in the centre of Paris and I was on Reception with people coming in or ringing non-stop. What about yours?"

"Don't ask," I reply and launch into a full account of the last few hours, hoping for a rush of sympathy.

She laughs.

"Oh, Mum, those are teething problems! Everyone has them when they move into a place."

"But Nikki," I protest, "I daren't even turn the water on without the boiler there. It could gush from anywhere. French plumbing is a complete mystery to me. So we can't flush the loo, clean our teeth or wash, as well as not being able to have coffee in the morning?"

"There's a bar down the road. All French bars sell coffee. And there's a patisserie opposite. Stop stressing, Mum and have some of this wine."

She pours the red liquid into two generous-sized plastic beakers and we steadily get so tipsy that my worries fade into the background…

What was that?

"Did you hear a tap on the door?" I ask.

"I hope it was," Nikki replies, "because that'll solve our water problems." She giggles.

"Nikki, you're beginning to sound like your dad," I reproach.

This time it's unmistakeable – someone *is* knocking on the door. Nikki gets up and opens it.

She returns with Marcel, who's dragging two foam mattresses lent by friends. He drops one in each room, kisses me on both cheeks and he and

Nikki return to his car to collect our belongings.

With Marcel's help we finish the wine. And when he leaves we slump onto the mattresses in our respective rooms. Within minutes I lose consciousness.

Chapter *Six*

"Wake up, Mum, I'm hungry."

I open my eyes from a disturbing, rapidly fading dream and squint at my watch.

"Nikki, it's only 7.15," I mumble.

"I've got to go to work and I need something to eat," she insists. "I can't go without my *petit déjeuner.*"

Unwashed and feeling grubby we go to the nearest bar, where Nikki orders *deux crèmes*, which she tells me is the more usual way of asking for *café au lait*. The plump, cheerful woman behind the bar seems to have taken an instant liking to Nikki. They're gabbling away like long-lost friends. She doesn't sell croissants but is happy for us to buy some from the patisserie and bring them here to eat with our coffee.

The smell coming from the bakery is irresistible – and we're certainly not about to resist! I treat us to *pains au chocolat* and we savour the still-warm, delicious pastries with freshly ground, piping hot coffee.

I begin to relax in the warmth of the bar, where a few men, presumably locals, are standing at the counter already drinking alcohol and laughing uproariously. Nikki says it's cheaper to drink standing but I'd rather pay the extra and sit at a table like we are.

"We must come back here soon," I say, as we pay and leave. "It's so friendly."

In the street, Nikki hugs me goodbye.

"I'm off to Ikea today," I tell her.

"Ok, Mum, but don't get anything for my room. I'd rather choose stuff for myself."

Since I already have my credit card on me, there's no reason to return to the cold, empty apartment.

"Hang on - I'll join you for part of the journey," I tell her as the bus arrives.

It's already crowded and we have to stand. Being retired I tend to forget that other people set off early for work.

We fare better on the Métro, where we manage to get seats together. At Gare du Nord we part company and I make my way towards the RER, the rail network that serves the suburbs. Several times I double back on myself – the signs here are extremely confusing. The scale of this ancient station is immense – it contains the Eurostar terminal, main lines to other parts of France, several Métro lines and the still-elusive RER – and to add to it all, this is rush hour. Hardly surprisingly I'm lost – I can lose my way coming out of a toilet.

I approach an elderly lady who looks as if she knows where she's going. She gives me a suspicious look as I begin with, "*Excusez-moi, Madame...*" Perhaps she thinks I'm one of the many people begging for money so often in evidence in Parisian stations.

I make her understand that I'm searching for the RER, she points out the direction and I continue my journey.

*

I'm waiting for the bus, utterly exhausted, bad-tempered and convinced I've forgotten something essential. The last four hours have made me wonder how anyone could actually *enjoy* shopping.

I've put several hundred pounds on my credit card and I'll have to wait two days for the delivery of my purchases.

As I emerge at last from our local Métro station, the *Mairie* clock tells me it's five o'clock. Although I've had enough of shopping there are still some vital necessities to buy. I dive into the nearest domestic appliance shop and, with a mixture of gestures and rapidly improving French, ask for their narrowest fridge/freezer, a gas cooker and the biggest, cheapest TV. Mercifully, he also accepts my card and promises delivery in the afternoon the day after tomorrow.

He asks me for the code to gain entry. I write it down and tell him I'm on the third floor, on the right hand side and warn him that the stairs are narrow and twisty.

"*Pas de problème, Madame.*"

He's probably used to this situation – there are many more apartments than houses in Paris, some, no doubt, with even twistier stairs than mine.

I thank him, buy two Chinese takeaways and hurry back to the apartment.

Nikki prattles on about her day as we eat, not appearing to notice that I'm past listening, that my eyes keep closing. And by nine o'clock I'm dozing off on my mattress, content for tomorrow to take care of itself.

*

It seems like I've slept for only a couple of hours before Nikki's persistent repetition of, "Mum…" puts an end to my beautiful dream. I was staying in the VIP suite of an exclusive, fashionable hotel in Paris, where, surrounded by the most sought-after plumbers, electricians, decorators and interior designers, I'd been offered their exclusive and immediate services. In a single day they'd transformed my tiny *pied-à-terre* into a spacious, sumptuous palace, complete with chandeliers, Chippendale furniture and illuminated fountains.

Squinting through half-open eyes, my hands touching cold, bare floorboards, I become aware that reality is an empty, whitewashed room. I want to retreat to the comfort of my dream…

"Get up, Mum, let's forage for our *petit déjeuner*," Nikki says cheerfully, putting on her coat. I can never understand her ability to welcome each day with such energy. It takes me a minimum of an hour to think coherently.

We chat as I'm dressing.

"Isn't it today that plumber guy's coming?"

"I hope so," I reply. "I don't want that boiler on the landing much longer. It's a miracle no one's complained yet. And I can't imagine how he's going to get it down that staircase. "

"That's his problem," Nikki retorts, then adds anxiously, "But are you sure you'll be safe with him on your own?"

This feels distinctly like role reversal.

"Oh yes, he even gave me his phone number.

It's totally above board."

"Let me see it," Nikki asks. She dials the number I give her and asks to speak to Luigi. A frown shows her puzzlement. "*Excusez-moi, Madame. Au revoir.*"

Ending the call, she looks at me, her face serious.

"Mum, he's given you a false number. There's no one there called Luigi. That was an old folks' home."

"Never mind, Nikki," I remark lightly, with a confidence I don't feel. "He wrote it in a hurry and probably made a mistake. I'll be absolutely fine. I'm a big girl now."

Rather than allow imagination to fuel my rapidly mounting anxiety about possibly spending a large part of today with a complete stranger, about whom I know nothing except that he's a plumber, I quickly change the subject.

"Right. I'm ready. Let's go, I'm ravenous." I'm don't want to admit that I'm actually feeling quite sick.

We go to the patisserie, then to the bar,

My struggle to eat my croissant goes unnoticed by Nikki, who's guzzled hers with obvious enjoyment and is now having a conversation with Martine, the amiable *proprietaire*.

Outside the apartment block, on the point of departing, she suddenly looks worried again.

"I think I'd better cancel work for today. I'll ring in and say I'm not well."

"No, Nikki," I say firmly. "You need the money and I need to learn to handle things here."

Reluctantly she concedes. But as I watch her bus disappear into the distance, I wish I'd let her stay.

Back in the apartment I start fretting again. What if this Italian Frenchman tries to attack me? I've got my mobile handy but I don't even know what the emergency number is. And anyway it probably wouldn't work on my English phone. The longer I'm here, the more I realise how much I'm going to have to learn and adapt if I'm going to survive.

A massive bang on the door makes me jump. My heart is racing as I go towards it. Through the spyhole I see Luigi with his toolbox.

I open the door and force a smile. "*Ah, bonjour, Luigi.*"

"*Bonjour, Madame,*" he grins back at me.

I stand back to let him enter. He places his toolbox on the kitchen floor, goes out onto the landing and heaves the boiler off the ground. Beads of sweat break out on his forehead as he slowly descends the staircase. He returns, panting heavily, with what I hope is a brand new replacement boiler. With great difficulty he places it on the kitchen floor before going back to his van. Looking out of the window I see him pull out a stepladder and bring it into the building

I watch in awe as he mounts the ladder and somehow manages to fix the unwieldy object into position, securing it tightly to the wall on a large mounting bracket.

Leaving him to carry on, I go into my bedroom and text Nikki to reassure her that so far, everything is going to plan. On my return to the kitchen Luigi already has the boiler wired in and connected to the water supply. He pulls the lever down ceremoniously to activate the water flow and we wait in silent anticipation as it fills up. In the next room the toilet starts flushing…

"*Voilà*!" he exclaims, clearly very proud of his handiwork.

"*Très bien! Merci beaucoup!*" I respond gratefully.

He turns it off again.

"*Ok, la toilette,*" he announces, turning off the water and making for the shower room, carrying what must be a flushing mechanism.

I feel ashamed as he wrinkles his nose at the stink emanating from the toilet – the unflushed results of my frequent nocturnal visits. He opens the window while I slink off into my bedroom to wait until he's finished the job.

"*Regardez, Madame!*" he calls.

In the shower room he demonstrates his success by pressing the metal button on top of the cistern. Thankfully the smell has now disappeared, along with the contents of the toilet.

I pay him the four hundred Euros he asks for the boiler, the toilet part and his labour with no idea whether this is a good bargain or I've been well and truly ripped off, but am simply content we can now use the water.

"*A demain.*" He shakes my hand, promising to return tomorrow afternoon to do the other jobs.

A wave of contentment floods through me as I close the door behind him and head towards the toilet for a celebratory pee.

Chapter *Sept*

I remember I forgot to buy a kettle. Right now I'd love a cup of tea. I make up my mind to walk briskly into town. With daily pastries and baguettes I'm fast losing my waistline. And there's no need to weigh myself to know I've put on weight because I feel too heavy for my legs. How do middle-aged French women manage to keep their slim figures? I go into the appliance shop.

"*Bonjour, Madame.*" The assistant remembers me. "*Je viens chez vous cet après-midi vers quinze heures.*"

So he's coming to my apartment this afternoon to deliver my goods at fifteen hours. I'm not very good at the twenty-four hour system but I think he means three o'clock.

Not knowing the word for kettle I point to the cheapest one I can see.

"*Une bouilloire!*" he informs me, placing it on the counter.

I pay for it, buy some tea and milk from the grocery next door, struggle back up the hill and reward myself by buying a tasty-looking raspberry tart and a salad baguette.

It's great to be back in my apartment, even in its present state. For the first time since childhood, I'm happy with simple things: running water, food, a working toilet and the means to make a hot drink, though not necessarily in that order.

Sitting cross-legged on my mattress I savour each sip of tea from my polystyrene cup, each mouthful of baguette and my exquisite dessert.

I lie back, contentedly full and wait for the deliveries.

*

A long way off a bell is ringing.

Surfacing slowly, I become aware that I must have dozed off. There's the sound again. And this time it's loud.

It's the doorbell.

No one's ever rung before. People always knock on my door. I'd even forgotten I had a bell.

I spring to my feet. Through the spyhole I see a couple of men with a mattress. I open the door.

"*Bonjour Madame. Ikea.*" Actually, I'd already worked that out from the bold letters on their jackets.

"*Bonjour, Messieurs.*"

I show them into my bedroom and ask them to place the mattress against the far wall.

They make several trips downstairs and by the time they've finished I have around a dozen boxes that almost fill the room to capacity. In fact, the flat-packed mezzanine bed has had to go into Nikki's room for the time being. The only recognizable items are the blue sofa bed, the folded shower curtain, the blue bubble-handled cutlery and four folding chairs.

I sign the form one of them hands me and with a quick "*Au revoir*", they disappear from sight.

I shut the door and stand staring at the boxes, wondering which to open first. I choose a smallish one, which contains everything required to build a crockery drainer. But DIY has never been my forte. The next box reveals a folding table with a large pack of screws, what looks like a range of white melamine planks and sheets of diagrams and instructions – in French, of course – to turn them into a table, a form of wizardry I've never yet attempted. I haven't even got a screwdriver.

Determined to prove to myself that I can turn my hand to some of this, I pick up the stainless steel rods that comprise the drainer and spread them out on the hall floor. Tackle one thing at a time, keep calm and this should be easy. No tools are needed for this job, merely commonsense. But as the minutes tick by, I doubt I've got any.

Just as I think I have every rod pushed into place, the top half of the drainer collapses. Only slightly deterred, I persevere and eventually, by paying more attention to the diagram, am able to view my completed achievement with pride.

A cursory inspection of the contents of a couple more boxes confirms that the revolving mirrored unit and the mezzanine bed are totally beyond my capabilities. However, the mention of a further monetary reward should persuade Luigi to put everything together.

This stuff will look great when it's built and in place, I think, trying to remain optimistic.

The doorbell again…

Throwing caution aside I open the door unchained. As I expected, it's Luigi, complete with cheeky grin and toolbox .

"*Bonjour, Madame.*"

I step backwards to allow him access to the

kitchen.

"*Il fait froid,*" I remark, rubbing my arms to illustrate my point. They taught us helpful phrases about the weather at school.

A blush spreads up from my neck to my face at his reply, which suggests that he could soon rectify the problem of feeling cold by warming us both up. And that smirk on his face means he's not referring to radiators.

Adopting a more formal approach now feels more appropriate, especially as he's made no move to start work – and I know the reputation of Italian men!

He looks up at the kitchen light, hanging precariously from its wire and I remind him it's the same in the shower room.

"*Oui, oui, Pas de problème!*" he exclaims. "I'm going to get my stepladder."

He goes out of the door I hadn't got round to closing.

While he's here I'd better look occupied. I don't want to encourage him by being too friendly.

I select a book from my suitcase about the best places to visit in Paris and sit browsing through it on one of the folding chairs in my bedroom.

Luigi's returned – at least, I hope it's him. And judging by noises in the kitchen he's started work.

I hear the stepladder being moved to the shower room. Slowly I unwind.

When Dennis arrives the apartment will be comfortably furnished and in perfect condition. We'll be able to spend our days seeing some famous sights. Dennis has been to Paris only once in his life and that was about thirty years ago. I'm really looking forward to Monday. And it's a mere three days away.

Luigi is standing in the doorway.

"Come and see what I've done," he beckons.

I follow him and sure enough, the lights are hanging as they should be and the exposed wires in the skirting boards in Nikki's room have been dealt with.

"*Merci, Luigi.* Would you like a cup of tea?" I offer politely as he proceeds to fix the wires in my room.

"Ah yes, the English always like their tea," he replies. "But no milk or sugar for me."

"Oh, and while you're here…" I try to sound casual. "There's some flat packed furniture that needs assembling." I show him the boxes and tell him what's inside. "How much more would you charge to do these?"

He scratches his head. "Shall we say another hundred Euros?" He's wearing a money-hungry expression.

Sure, I think, you say a hundred if you like. "Eighty. That's the most I can afford."

"Ok, eighty then," he concedes.

Brewing the tea in polystyrene beakers, I make a mental note to buy crockery.

Taking Luigi's tea to him I'm astounded to see the tall revolving unit nearly assembled. He's clearly an incredibly fast worker. I'd best leave him to it …

Picking up my book I go into Nikki's room.

Looking at pictures of the *Louvre* I note that

entrance is free to the greatest public museums and art galleries on the first Sunday of every month. So in little over a week we could be touring one of the largest and grandest museums in the world, admiring some of the most famous sculptures and paintings in existence.

The following day we'll return to England, leaving Nikki to run (preferably not *ruin*) the apartment and hopefully keep it clean. I've already told her she can do whatever she likes in her own room but not to allow anyone to smoke or use the bed in mine. She's not expected to pay rent but I do expect her to pay the gas, electricity and phone bills - she's already informed me she's having a landline installed. I've also asked her to foot the bill for the quarterly charges that each apartment owner pays towards the maintenance of the building.

Hours pass with the sounds of Luigi beavering away. He appears in the doorway at five o'clock (or seventeen hours French time) and urges me to inspect the results of his labours. I'm thrilled to see my room with fully built furniture.

He apologises for not having time to tackle the table but I assure him that if he lends me a screwdriver, I'll have no trouble putting that together (am I kidding myself or him?).

"I will come back on Sunday and take you to *Leroy Merlin*. That is a very large shop where you can buy any sort of *bricolage*..."

"*Bricolage?*" That's a new word to me. And I was doing so well understanding him until now.

With further explanation and the inevitable waving of hands, he conveys the meaning of the word – *Bricolage* is Do-It-Yourself! *Leroy Merlin* is the French equivalent of a B & Q store.

"That is where you can buy your a rail for the shower curtain and choose a radiator to put beside the toilet. And it's cheap," he adds

What does he call cheap? I understand the meaning of cheap in England but have no idea of relative costs in France.

I thank him and see him out, knowing he'll return as he's not yet been paid.

And when he does I'll have to ask him if he'll do one last, important job. I'd completely forgotten about the mezzanine stored temporarily in Nikki's room.

At half past six Nikki bounces in brimming with excitement. She's been offered a full time position with the firm she's temping for. Apparently, the boss is really impressed with her French and her excellent PR skills.

"Fantastic, darling! That's excellent news. The day's gone well for me, too. Ikea delivered everything and Luigi has assembled most of the furniture. My only worry is whether the kitchen appliances will materialise. They were supposed to be delivered this afternoon and it's getting rather late."

"Mum," Nikki reproaches, "you've got to get used to the way they do things here. They're probably waiting till closing time before bringing them."

"Then why did he say they'd be here around three o'clock?"

"Maybe he's short staffed. You worry far too

much. Chill out, Mum."

She's right. Odd thumping sounds on the stairs herald their arrival.

"*Bonsoir, Madame.*"

Two beefy, red-faced men manoeuvre their way with surprising ease into the kitchen with a fridge freezer, placing it in the alcove and adjusting its feet to prevent it rocking on the uneven floor tiles.

Next comes the gas cooker, which they connect to the mains pipe, and finally the television.

"We've brought you an aerial, too, at no extra charge," one says, holding it up in front of my nose.

"*Merci beaucoup.*"

I show him where to put the television – almost touching the ceiling and directly opposite where I plan to have the mezzanine. He looks at me as though I've landed from another planet, but they carry out my instructions, pushing furniture aside to make room for their stepladder and drilling deep holes in the wall to support an enormous platform for the bulky, large-screen television. Hopefully, it won't ever come crashing down. If it does, it will probably end up in the apartment below.

I sign their worksheet and see them out.

"Good for you, Mum," Nikki praises. "You handled that perfectly, without any help from me."

Over a takeaway pizza, which my cheeky daughter phoned to be delivered from the shop directly opposite, we exchange detailed events of our day.

"Let's watch my TV," I suggest.

We sit on a corner of my mattress, craning our

necks.

I don't understand a word of the comedy show Nikki's laughing at. The speed of their speech is unbelievably fast and it's probably colloquial, too. I quickly become bored. Have I paid out good money for this?

As soon as the programme finishes, it's bedtime for me.

This room looks like a storage area at the back of a shop. There's just about enough space for me on the mattress. Perhaps I've bought too much, thinking of what I needed rather than what would fit.

Ah well, time enough to sort that out tomorrow.

Within seconds, I'm asleep.

Chapter *Huit*

I'm up and ready for my breakfast. As it's Saturday, Nikki sleeps on, no doubt tired out after her week's work.

I buy croissants for us both and nip into the grocery shop on the ground floor of our block. As well as buying a jar of instant coffee and some basic groceries, I exchange a few pleasantries with the jovial little man behind the counter. This is the kind of shop you could once find in any English town before the advent of the supermarket. There are still plenty in and around Paris.

Enjoying my croissants and coffee, I reflect that my confidence and competence with the French language are increasing daily. I've ceased worrying if I make mistakes and am generally able to convey what I want to say and understand the reply. And it feels good. I also get the impression that Parisians are pleased that I'm making an effort to converse with them in their own language. We English speakers have a reputation for expecting the rest of the world to speak *our* language.

With no specific plans for this morning, I'm going to attempt to assemble the table. I empty the box and lay out the pieces on the hall floor. This shouldn't prove too difficult.

My enthusiasm gradually ebbs away as I pore intently over the booklet of complicated looking diagrams, searching for a starting point. It's taking me ages to summon up enough courage to begin.

I pick up Luigi's screwdriver and, using what I hope are the correct sized screws, join piece to piece according to my interpretation of the illustrations, keenly aware that if there are more ways than one of doing anything, I'm likely to choose the wrong one. Nevertheless, my self-esteem rises as the various bits begin to assume the shape of a drop-leaf table – and I'm not put off by occasionally having to unscrew parts I've joined incorrectly.

Standing back to view my achievement, I choose to disregard the fact that the drawers at each end of the table have to be opened carefully to avoid pulling them right out. But why is there such a large assortment of screws left over? Perhaps the French are more generous about this kind of thing. Dennis usually discovers he's several screws short (as I keep telling him!). He invariably blames it on what he terms the "Friday Afternoon" pack.

I gingerly move the table against my bedroom wall to provide further support if it does collapse. Nikki appears, rubbing the sleep from her eyes, which widen when she sees what I've accomplished. She's never seen an example of my DIY skills – probably because I've never used them before. And for once she's speechless.

Proudly, I demonstrate the miracle that makes the flap nearest us stay up in a horizontal position. We eat lunch – or in Nikki's case, brunch – sitting on chairs at my newly completed table. How civilized this feels! I hide my suspicion that the table is held together mainly by my faith in it and that if I stop believing, it will give way and deposit our food on the floor.

"Nikki, what are you doing this afternoon? I have to buy crockery and a number of other essentials."

"Let's spend the afternoon together then, because I desperately need some new clothes."

"What about your room? Aren't you going to buy *anything* for it?"

"Yes, of course. But that can wait till I've painted it."

"Oh," I remark as casually as I can. "What colour?"

"Midnight blue," she answers.

Is she serious?

"Ok," I say slowly, resisting the temptation to criticise her choice of colour, reminding myself that it's her room, at least until she can afford a place to rent, so I mustn't interfere.

We leave the apartment and Nikki takes me to *Les Halles*, a giant, semi-underground shopping complex and major Métro interchange, at *Chatelet*, in the heart of the city.

"There's every kind of shop you could wish for, Mum," she calls to me as we weave our way between crowds of people.

Personally, I'd hoped for somewhere less noisy and densely populated.

We visit several chic clothes shops where Nikki tries on a number of outfits. I'm fast tiring of hanging about outside changing rooms, waiting to be consulted on each and every garment. Perhaps this is how Dennis feels when I drag *him* out clothes shopping…

Nikki selects a pair of jeans with designer slits in them, ignoring my offer to cut her present pair for free. While I'm waiting, I approach an assistant.

"*Excusez-moi, quelle heure est-il?*"

"*Bonjour, Madame,*" she says stiffly, with the emphasis on the first word and a sour look on her face. "*Il est seize heures dix.*"

Perhaps she thinks it's time I got a watch.

Nikki pays for her jeans, ignoring my failure to share her happiness about them.

"Nikki," I whisper, "I can't understand why almost everyone I've spoken to since I've been in Paris either scowls at me or says *bonjour* very pointedly. I try to be polite and begin my request with "excuse me"."

"Mum, that's something else you must learn. No matter who you approach in a shop, a bar or wherever, it's an unwritten Parisian courtesy that before you say anything else you start with *bonjour* or, if it's evening, *bonsoir*. They'll be far more willing to help if you remember that."

Problem solved at last. I was beginning to get rather paranoid.

"Nikki, it's already ten past four and I haven't bought anything I intended to get. How about we split up for a couple of hours? We could meet up at half past six." I look quickly at all the shops within spitting range. "At *Quick*," I suggest, recognising the familiar sign of a chain of French fast-food restaurants.

"That's fine with me," she answers cheerfully.

Going at my own pace, I meander along until one particular shop catches my attention. Initially I'm attracted by the window display of novelty teapots, ornamented cups and several types of tea. Emblazoned below one of the windows in large gold lettering I read, *"COMPAGNIE ANGLAISE DES THES"* – English Tea Company. Once inside I discover a tea-drinker's paradise, shelves stacked high with colourful tins, intricately decorated china mugs and packets of tea from countries worldwide. There's even a complete set for a Japanese tea ceremony.

This shop has dispelled my notion that the French drink nothing but coffee, alcohol and mineral water. Or is it perhaps another tourist attraction?

A magnificent aroma hangs in the air. It's hard to define but there's a sweetness of strawberries mixed with the sharpness of citrus fruits.

A closer look at some of the tins reveals some unusual flavours of tea, like Banana, Tutti Frutti and some labelled in English like Apple Pie. This is certainly not your typical traditional English Tea Shoppe!

I pick up a metal mesh ball attached to a chain, obviously some kind of infuser. You have to undo the catch, fill the ball with loose tea, close it and dunk it in boiling water to brew.

"*Bonjour*," I begin, dangling the strainer in front of an assistant and somehow conveying to her that I haven't a clue how to open it.

She smiles at me – she actually smiles at me! Nikki was right: *Bonjour* works perfectly!

She demonstrates how to undo the catch and then at my request weighs and packages a hundred grams of apricot tea.

"Is this really an English company?"

"No, Madame, it's French."

But of course, it makes sense to make it sound English, as we're famous for our daily cuppa.

I choose a couple of exquisite bone china mugs, pay for my goods and leave the shop.

Instead of buying the necessities I came out for, I've used a considerable amount of time and money indulging my curiosity for new experiences. Never mind, I'm enjoying it.

I seek out a kitchenware shop. The crockery, however, is overly fancy and way beyond my fast-diminishing budget. I'm beginning to realise that this whole area caters largely for the luxury rather than the utilitarian market. So for tonight's meal it will be paper plates and expensive mugs. I resolve to venture into my local area, where there are plenty of small shops filled with heavily discounted items of every description.

As Dennis is insisting on bringing out his CD player, I go into a music shop and come out with a handful of CDs of my choice of music.

I ask another shopper the time (I took off my watch forever when I retired), prefacing my request, of course, with, "*Bonjour...*"

It's five minutes before our rendezvous and I'm lost again. Still, somebody here will know the general direction of *Quick*...

I arrive via a series of directions and misdirections to find Nikki shuffling impatiently from one foot to the other with yet more designer clothes judging from the bags she's carrying.

What a relief to sit, enjoy a coffee and ease my aching feet! Idly, I contemplate the oddities of language. The French must have an enormous vocabulary to draw on but they prefer an English word for this fast-food restaurant – or is it the American influence? And on their menus they offer such delicacies as 'Les Chicken Wings', 'Le Curry' and 'Le Crumble'. I've noticed another chain of restaurants called *Flunch.* Does that mean "Fast Lunch"?

"Come on," I urge Nikki, who, clearly revelling in her purchases, is examining each one in minute detail. "Time we were going home." Already I'm thinking of my little apartment as *home*.

But the immensely confusing maze of passages and levels makes it difficult for even Nikki to find the way to the Métro Line we want. It's several wrong turns before we find ourselves on a moving walkway, which takes us towards Line 1, direction *Chateau de Vincennes* on the first leg of our journey back.

We buy a Turkish takeaway when we emerge at our destination.

Nikki looks as exhausted as I feel. After supper we admire each other's purchases and half a bottle of wine later kiss each other goodnight.

As usual, sleeps soon engulfs me.

Chapter *Neuf*

It's as well that I'm rudely awakened by Nikki.

"Aren't you up yet, Mum? I thought Luigi was taking you to *Leroy Merlin* today. Anyway, it's a lovely sunny morning and I'm off to spend the day with Marcel."

I sit bolt upright, suddenly alert and anxious.

"What if he arrives the moment you go? I can't let him see me like this. It might give him the wrong idea."

"Ok, I'll make us a coffee. But please hurry up, I haven't got much time."

That's my daughter, forever in a rush.

We drink our coffee without talking, sitting on Nikki's mattress with the sun streaming through the window. I feel that, hard though it is making this apartment comfortable, we are so lucky to have found it. Ever since I set foot in its narrow hallway I've sensed a calmness, a stillness throughout. There's a peaceful atmosphere here that is comforting. We haven't talked about this but, seeing her relaxed expression, I think Nikki feels it too.

The doorbell shatters the silence.

"It's either Marcel or Luigi," Nikki decides, on her way to find out.

"*C'est qui?*" she calls out.

"Marcel," a deep voice replies from the other side of the door.

Nikki lets him in. I join them in the hallway.

"*Bonjour, Madame Fielding.*"

We go through the formality of the kissing

routine, once on each cheek. Most of Nikki's friends shake my hand on the first encounter and after that some of them kiss me twice, a few kiss me four times and occasionally it's three. I'm confused. It's a ritual I haven't yet got used to. But I follow the other person's lead.

"It depends where they come from," Nikki explained vaguely when I questioned her about this custom of greeting people you scarcely know. "It's usually twice for Paris."

Nikki puts on her coat while Marcel and I chat about the weather – safe ground for someone English! Perhaps the French think this is the limit of our conversational ability. Or maybe they think it's the English equivalent of their kissing routine.

Nikki smiles at Marcel. "Let's go," she says, fidgeting with her gloves.

They both kiss me goodbye. The gesture is as automatic as the Americans' "Have a good day".

On her way out, Nikki throws me a warning.

"By the way, Mum, be careful. Can you really trust a man who gives you a fake phone number?"

"I appreciate your concern, Nikki, but I can handle the situation. He's probably being cautious because he's working for me on the black."

Closing the door behind them I decide that, having coped so well with this kissing business, I deserve another coffee. I'm filling the kettle when the bell rings again.

"*C'est qui?*" I enquire loudly.

"*C'est Luigi, le plombier.*"

Well *he's* not getting any kisses from me. I release the locks.

We exchange *bonjour*s and I make room for him to enter.

But he doesn't.

"Are you ready, Madame?" he asks.

"Oh, er, *oui*," I reply, hastily grabbing my coat.

Coffee will have to wait.

His expression conveys his impatience to get moving.

It's chilly outside. I fasten my buttons and pull up the collar. Luigi points to a small, whitish van, its hazard lights flashing, parked dangerously on a bend to one side of a pedestrian crossing. I sigh, remembering many other similarly parked vehicles in Paris. How do they get away with it?

I add this to my list of reasons why I'll never take up driving here.

Luigi opens the passenger door for me to squeeze into the seat beside him. The door panel is missing, exposing the interior workings. But this is a minor fault compared with other, more serious signs of deterioration and neglect. Like the smashed door mirrors and the wires dangling below the dashboard.

I shuffle my feet carefully to find a place for them amid the bottles, cans, cigarette cartons and papers littering the floor.

It takes several tries before Luigi succeeds in starting the engine of his four-wheeled dustbin. He moves quickly up through the gears and speeds off through the suburbs, humming to himself, passing within inches of an old man wobbling on a bicycle. Buildings and parks flash by.

I shiver, more from fearful anticipation than

from cold. Luigi is clearly a mobile accident looking for somewhere to happen. I feel dreadfully sick. I close my eyes, reopening them as the van slows to a stop.

"*Voilà! Leroy Merlin!*" Luigi announces, jerking on the handbrake.

"*Merci,*" I say shakily. Dare I even risk the return journey?

Inside the store Luigi steers me swiftly through the numerous aisles, seeming to know precisely where he's going. He stops in front of a vast array of radiators.

"Here's the electric heater you need." He lifts down a compact white device from the shelf and dumps it in the trolley. Seizing this golden opportunity, I smile sweetly and persuade him to add a freestanding oil radiator. Probably to pre-empt any further demands he moves us on swiftly towards the lighting area, where he picks out two electric light covers with metal guards, assuring me that these are waterproof, perfect for the kitchen and shower-room.

Luigi keeps looking around in a decidedly furtive manner. Is he perhaps worried that a wife, girlfriend or taxman might spot him?

He hurries me towards the bathroom fittings and consults his watch.

"We must go soon" His eyes continually dart to left and right.

"Here's your shower rail," he says, grabbing one from the display. How can he tell it's the right size? Ah well, I expect he knows what he's doing. And if he doesn't I'm not about to annoy him by asking.

He's scurrying towards a checkout with the trolley but there's a long queue so I know I've got a few minutes before I have to join him. I rush off randomly round the store, seizing a new toilet seat, two lampshades for my bedroom and the hallway and an unusual table lamp shaped like a chest of drawers with a light on top.

Approaching the checkout with my arms full, I catch sight of Luigi's furious expression. I know he's anxious to leave but I can't let slip this chance to accumulate more "necessities" for the apartment. And anyway, he's stuck in a slow moving queue so what's the problem?

I intercept a shelf-stacker before he can escape, knowing that when you need one, store assistants are as rare as duck's toenails.

"*Bonjour, Monsieur.* Can you tell me where I can find cupboards for under and over my shower room sink?"

He frowns. I repeat my request loudly but he still doesn't understand. So putting down my goods I begin a series of actions, which include lots of bending, stretching and elaborate shape making with my hands, interspersed with the best French I can muster. I'm desperate to communicate my message but when I'm edgy the right words fail me.

The open-mouthed assistant waves a hand vaguely towards the back of the store before returning to his task. His meaning is obvious: "That's someone else's department. Go and ask them."

I risk a sideways glance at Luigi. He's clearly

ready to explode.

I dash towards the rear of the building, where an enormous variety of cupboards are on display. Scanning the shelves quickly I catch sight of exactly what I want, available in flat packs but much too heavy and bulky for me, especially on top of what I'm already carrying.

There's only one thing for it. Returning to the as yet unexploded Luigi I cajole him into following me back down the store. I'm sure the only reason he's complying is that he knows I'm paying him well! But even so, I can see from his face how he feels about it.

He slams the packs onto the trolley and mutters something in Italian under his breath about the English. I'm glad I can't hear the whole of it.

"Ok, that's it" I announce. "I've finished."

But Luigi, without allowing me another second to continue my shopping spree, has already set off in the direction of the checkouts. I have to trot to keep track of him.

Parisians may not queue for buses but they certainly do in shops – and how!

"*Merde!*" Luigi grunts, his eyes flicking constantly to everyone around him. I wish he'd stop doing this; I'm beginning to feel like we're a couple of escaped convicts.

A heavy silence hangs between us during the half hour it takes to pay, exit the store and load the stuff into his van.

And Luigi takes his revenge on the return journey with a spectacular display of Parisian driving at its most hair-raising, while I try not to further soil the already dirty passenger seat.

In the relative safety of my compartment I relax enough to speak.

"Would you like a coffee, Luigi?" My French flows easily now I'm on my own territory.

He nods curtly, already halfway up his stepladder to fit the shower rail.

I pretend to busy myself, endlessly rearranging things in my suitcase until Luigi calls me. His mood, in keeping with his Italian temperament, suddenly and unexpectedly changes as I go from room to room admiring his work – the shower rail is fixed, the radiator's in place and the waterproof light shields are secured to the shower and kitchen ceilings. He's even put up my bedroom and hall light shades. He's beaming, obviously very proud of his efforts. It's like the sun coming out after heavy rain.

I daren't mention the packs containing the cupboards as I have a bigger favour to ask him. I can always surprise Dennis by suggesting *he* tries to use any practical talents I'm not aware of.

"*Bravo, Luigi!* Could you do one more thing for me?" I request timidly.

I feel compelled to ask him to help me assemble the mezzanine because Dennis will be here tomorrow and I'm keen to impress him with my achievements. But however good the apartment looks, the lack of a decent bed to sleep in would prove terribly disappointing for someone who claims that getting into bed at night is the moment he's been waiting for ever since he got up.

Luigi smiles, somewhat slyly, taking several

steps towards me.

I retreat until my back touches the hall wall.

"Could you please help me put up the mezzanine?" My voice rises to a pleading squeak. "I'll give you fifty Euros on top of what I already owe you," I add quickly, noting the deepening furrow in his brow.

The money does the trick.

"Ok. But when it's done we have to try it out," he says softly. "We have to kiss and cuddle."

I laugh nervously and wave my wedding ring in front of his eyes, resisting the urge to knee him in the groin. A randy Italian is not what I need.

"I'm married," I say, stating the obvious.

"It makes no difference to me," Luigi replies with a glint in his eye.

"Well it does to me. I love my husband, so no!" I retaliate firmly. What I don't tell him is that I wouldn't fancy him even if I were single.

If I'd slapped his face he couldn't look more taken aback.

"Well, you're the first married woman I know to refuse."

I detect a slight shift in his attitude, an air of respect that was lacking previously.

Luigi, ignoring the instruction booklet, figures out by trial and error, and with the aid of the occasional "*Merde!*", his own method of assembling this towering structure. My job is to support various metal rods whilst he joins others on. It's finally done, complete with a narrow ladder to its dizzy heights. As we hoist the heavy mattress into place, Luigi can't resist a further attempt to woo me. But this time it's lukewarm, probably his idea of a joke. I simply smile.

I pay him in full and he leaves. And I'll never see him again.

Heaving a huge sigh I climb the rungs, stretch out on my mattress, lean over the safety rail and switch on the television, which I'm delighted to notice perfectly matches the height of the bed, and watch children's cartoons.

Chapter *Dix*

My alarm clock's buzzing.

That was an exceptionally comfortable night's sleep, snuggled up on my elevated bed. I climb carefully backwards down the ladder and fold back the shutters allowing Monday morning to filter into my bedroom. It's important to make an early start today, as there are a fair number of finishing touches left to do. I want to put a big smile on Dennis' face at the end of his journey.

Washed and dressed, I set off for the patisserie, an autumnal spring in my step. The aroma of freshly baked goodies wafts towards me as I cross the road to join the lengthening queue inside the bakery.

"*Bonjour, Monsieur,*" I say when it's my turn.

The baker greets me with the friendliness he reserves for regular customers. "Same as usual?"

I nod, he selects two fluffy *pains au chocolat*.

He says, *"Bonne journée*" and I wish him a good day too.

I return to my apartment with our *petit déjeuner*, fondly imagining that I'm now a fully-fledged *Parisienne*.

Nikki never likes being woken but her mood softens when I present her with newly-baked pastries and steaming hot coffee. Turning on her blow heater, I make a mental note to ask Dennis to bring the one from our spare room.

"Nikki, is there anything you'd like me to ask Dad to bring out for you?"

She considers the question for a moment.

"I'd love some Bisto and Marmite," she says. "You can't get them here."

You probably can't but I bet she wouldn't know what to do with them if you could. I know who's going to be using them to prepare a meal and it won't be Nikki. She has many talents but cooking isn't one of them.

I'm washing up when Nikki embraces me and hurries out.

"Don't forget you're meeting Dad at *Gare du Nord* tonight," I call after her. "And I'll have supper waiting for you both."

By a quarter to nine I'm in town and dismayed to discover that a lot of the shops don't open until ten. I suppose that's because they stay open longer at night.

I sit in a corner of a bar with a coffee. My caffeine levels must be soaring. Perhaps that's how I'm able to keep up such a hectic lifestyle here.

I dial Dennis' number on my mobile.

"Why are you ringing so early?" he mumbles, clearly half asleep.

"Oh, sorry, love! I forgot we're an hour ahead of you."

"So what's the problem?"

"Nothing. Just ringing to ask you to bring a small heater, a couple of continental adapters, the wall clock in the loft – oh, and Nikki would like some Bisto and Marmite." It all comes out in one breath.

"And a partridge in a pear tree?" he responds sarcastically. "Don't they sell *anything* out there? Sounds distinctly uncivilized to me."

"Look, Dennis, I'm running out of time, money and patience. Pack what you can and leave the rest. And have a good trip," I add curtly, ending the call. Hardly the ideal recipe for the start of our week together, for what I was hoping would turn out to be a second honeymoon.

Not to worry, I reassure myself. Wait until he sees how homely I've made our little investment – well, little sizewise! Dennis knows the state it was in initially but not a lot else. Hopefully, he'll be tickled pink by my attempts at interior design.

I order another coffee and run through my to-do list for this morning – open bank account, buy mugs, plates, pans, flowers, a rug…

But food for this evening comes first, bearing in mind that Dennis' diet is based around chicken, chips and baked beans. He's not one for experimenting with new dishes – in fact, he's stubbornly resistant to the mere suggestion. I can foresee decided difficulties with finding places to eat out in this city renowned for and proud of its own cuisine.

I leave the warmth of the bar to brave the cold weather and approach an elderly woman with a shopping trolley in tow,

"*S'il vous plaît, Madame.*" I'm using "please" this time instead of "hello" – Nikki says it's an equally acceptable approach. "I'm English and I'm a stranger here. Can you tell me a cheap place to buy groceries?"

"*Ah, Anglaise!* Your best place is *Ed*," she replies. "It's one of the cheaper supermarkets. I'm going there myself so I'll show you where it is."

"*Merci, Madame.*" I match my pace with her painfully slow steps.

"*Il fait froid*," I remark.

She nods but shows no inclination for conversation about the weather, or anything else for that matter. Looking at her trolley I promise myself I'll buy one. It's a must or *le must* as I've heard Nikki say when referring to the latest fashion accessory. *Franglais*, a mixture of French and English, is definitely *à la mode* here.

Inside *Ed*, with Dennis' restrictive menu firmly in mind, I settle for chicken pieces, potato wedges and frozen peas.

I spend the next two hours and a pocketful of Euros buying everything else on my list and a shopping trolley to hold it. How readily Euros flow out. They feel like Mickey Mouse money.

Before I return to the apartment I must open a bank account. In an inside pocket of my coat are my passport, proof of address and a plastic wallet bulging with money, which I'd rather not be looking after myself.

*

I can't understand why none of the banks seems to want my money. I thought opening an account would be easy but there's more to it than I realised. However, one helpful bank clerk suggested the Post Office. Bingo! I had all the right paperwork, their charges are minimal and they've lifted the burden of carrying my worldly wealth around Paris.

I catch a bus back, heave my overloaded trolley onto the pavement and wait for the traffic to stop at the pedestrian crossing – which it doesn't. In frustration I place an experimental foot onto the crossing and a car screeches to a standstill. Ah, so that's how it's done!

The trolley loses its usefulness at the bottom of the stairs up to my apartment. It's too unwieldy. Leaving it in the foyer I force my tired legs up the three flights with the rug and return for another load. After four trips my hallway is full and I've had more than enough exercise for one day. I reckon I've already compensated for the delicious strawberry and kiwi tarts I'm about to tuck into with a nice cup of tea.

The afternoon passes quickly as I clean, arrange and rearrange rooms. I close Nikki's door, partly to respect her privacy but mainly because the layers of mess on her floor spoil the tranquil image I've worked hard to create.

Supper's in the oven, the table's laid and I'm putting the final touches to what is now my lounge-cum-bedroom, when I hear loud bumping, clumping sounds on the stairs. They undoubtedly herald the arrival of Nikki and Dennis.

The door bursts open and a dishevelled Dennis stumbles into the hall, dragging an enormous suitcase. Nikki takes up the rear, struggling with his backpack and holdall.

"Those stairs'll be the death of me," he gasps breathlessly.

Not quite the entry I'd envisaged for our reunion.

"Do you mean 'Hello, darling, nice to see you'?"

"Sorry, love." He leans forward to kiss me then peers into the kitchen. "Bit small, isn't it?"

"I wish I'd photographed it the day we moved in," I say wistfully.

Dennis has moved on to the shower room.

"You've done a good job in here," he declares. "But the door won't shut and I need the toilet. So close your ears." He sounds irritated.

Nikki and I try not to listen to the sound of Dennis peeing. She smiles at me sympathetically.

"He's worn out from travelling, Mum."

Dennis reappears.

"That's better, " he sighs.

I fling open the door to the bedroom, my *pièce de résistance*, where soft lighting illuminates my efforts.

"Ah, now this is lovely. You really…" His jaw drops open. "You're surely not expecting me to sleep up there, are you?" he challenges.

Without answering, I retreat to the kitchen to hide my tears of disappointment. When I emerge with supper, Dennis moves towards me and hugs me tightly.

"I'm sorry. I've had a proper look. You've done wonders with this little flat."

I feel myself mellowing as he continues.

"And you've cooked a good English meal, something I can get my teeth into. None of that *haute cuisine* I was afraid you might serve up."

Nikki and I laugh.

Happily, Dennis' good humour, fuelled by a

generous glass of cognac, continues throughout the evening, even failing to be dampened by his head making audible contact with the ceiling on our midnight ascent to loftier heights.

Chapter *Onze*

Despite the occasional moan about seasickness (perhaps the bed's swaying because Luigi didn't tighten the bolts sufficiently) Dennis' cheerful mood appears to have survived the night. He's noticeably relaxed over his bowl of muesli.

After breakfast he reveals the contents of his suitcase. Electrical equipment, warm clothing for us both, a variety of food and drink and numerous other sundries spill out onto the floor.

I watch open-mouthed.

"Dennis, this looks like a long-term survival kit. We're in France, not the Antarctic. They do have normal shops here," I remonstrate.

"Well, you asked me to bring some of it. And for the rest it's best to be on the safe side," he retorts defensively.

Whilst I try to find storage space for everything, Dennis sets to work assembling my bathroom furniture.

Amazingly, it takes a mere couple of hours to complete our respective tasks. And finally I'm able to store my makeup under the sink and use the mirror on the wall cupboard above to apply it.

Sipping coffee, Dennis produces a passport sized photo of himself from an inside pocket.

"I even remembered to bring this," he announces, handing it to me.

"Looks like a police mugshot. Never mind, at least we can get you an Orange Card for the Métro. But first I need to go to the supermarket. I'm running out of soya milk."

“Milk comes from mammals. Since when has the soya bean been a mammal?” he quips.

After thirty years of marriage I’m used to his dry wit.

We venture out into the bright, sunny street and make our way to the nearest supermarket. Before we enter, I hiss in Dennis’ ear.

“Be careful what you say in here. Parisians may not appear to speak English but a lot of them understand it. And if you make any derogatory comments about the French they probably won’t know you’re joking.”

“Why would I be joking?”

“You know what I mean!”

“Yus, Miss!” He puts on his naughty schoolboy expression.

Food shopping is, for me, an activity to be accomplished as fast as possible. Dennis maintains he feels likewise, yet invariably manages to collect a huge number of items on his systematic tour of the aisles. Today is no exception.

“Unless you want to spend the rest of the day here, I suggest we join the checkout queue.”

Reluctantly he follows me, carrying a basket overflowing with non-essentials. But at least he’s managed to find things he’ll eat, like sliced bread, biscuits, cakes, crisps…

At last it’s my turn. I place my armful of goods on the conveyor belt. The assistant checks them through so quickly that she fails to hear me attempting to draw her attention to Dennis’ basketload.

“I’m paying for all of these,” I repeat,

indicating his items.

She heaves a huge sigh as she scans his goods.

I fumble through my purse for the money.

"Look, you're keeping the whole queue waiting," she snaps irritably.

I feel my colour heighten as I pay. We hurriedly pack our shopping into bags and make a speedy exit to avoid further embarrassment.

"What was all that about?" Dennis asks.

I explain what happened as we walk back to the apartment.

"How rude," he says. "Typically - "

"Typically nothing!" I interrupt. "They're not all like that. Even in England you get unhelpful shop assistants. It's nothing to do with being French."

"I'll believe it when I see it," he mutters.

I hope I'll be able to prove my point before too long.

Remembering Nikki's advice about climbing the fifty-one steps to the apartment rapidly, rather than prolong the agony, I attempt what feels like a sprint but is probably more like a determined plod, pausing briefly on each landing to regain my breath.

I unlock the door and wait for Dennis, who arrives minutes later, bowed down with carrier bags, puffing, blowing and looking close to collapse.

I revive him with soup and toast but it does make me wonder how we'll cope in a decade or two.

"Nikki's friend mentioned a shopping centre not far from here," I remark cheerfully.

"Apparently there's a C&A there. They still exist over here. It might be worth a visit after lunch."

Dennis' slow, non-committal nod reinforces the lack of enthusiasm on his face. He knows I like shopping for clothes; he enjoys it about as much as he'd enjoy having his teeth removed with a pair of pliers.

We walk to the Métro, where I buy our weekly passes.

"These cover us for buses as well as trains," I say, guiding him to the bus stop, where we surge forward with a crowd battling for space on an already packed bus. We manage to squeeze on, to Dennis' all-too-obvious disappointment.

"Move further down the bus," the driver commands as everyone squashes ever more tightly together. We're closer to complete strangers than we would be to intimate friends and family in this giant tinful of people. A baguette is forcing itself into my ear.

Sweat breaks out on my forehead as claustrophobia sets in. Through the crush of bodies I glimpse a steady trail of would-be travellers continuing to force their way on.

I'm fighting to control my panic as the doors finally close. The bus pulls away and begins a painful uphill crawl, repeatedly slowing almost to a halt. Surprisingly, we not only make it to the next stop but actually find seats shortly before our destination.

Dennis looks decidedly disgruntled. "I haven't had so much fun since -"

"- you fell off your moped," I interrupt,

completing one of his inevitable remarks after an incident that displeases him.

But it breaks the ice and we stroll hand in hand to the shopping centre. With its huge variety of shops and eating-places on two levels, well lit, clean throughout and with conveniently situated free toilets, it's something akin to my idea of heaven.

Dennis is lured into a massive haven of technology called *Fnac*, whilst I indulge my passion for good-quality, reasonably priced clothes in C&A…

I look at the time – has an hour passed already? As if on cue, Dennis arrives.

"Coffee time," he suggests. "There's a place nearby called *Brioche Dorée* where there are some nice-looking French tarts. And you know how much I like tarts." He sniggers.

I flash him a wry smile.

There is indeed a scrumptious selection of pastries at the café as well as excellent coffee. Dennis is impressed, too. As ever, I think, the way to a man's heart is via his stomach.

At one end of this *Centre Commercial* is a superstore called *Carrefour*. We're both curious to find out what's on offer here. But to get past the security guards involves having our bags inspected and sealed up – presumably so we can't slip anything into them. I can sense Dennis working up to a sarcastic comment and give him what I hope is a suitably warning look.

Every shop has security guards. A sign of the times, I suppose!

This place sells almost anything from vintage

wines to car accessories. And Dennis takes a great deal of convincing that we can't stay here until closing time. Bargain hunting is one of his hobbies There are more checkouts than I've ever seen in one store – and furthermore, they're all open, each one with its everlasting queue. As is usually the case, the one we join turns out to be the slowest – but experience has long since taught me that if I change queues, the next one will be even worse.

"Dennis, I meant to buy some packets of soup. Would you mind nipping back and picking a few up? Something thick and nourishing."

"Ok," he says. "Anything rather than stand in a queue going nowhere."

He disappears from sight and I content myself with people watching…

Having reached the front I'm looking round anxiously for Dennis He'd better be here soon…

"*Bonjour Madame*."

"*Bonjour,*" I reply automatically.

The girl begins to scan my goods. The man behind me smiles.

"Would your husband like to come in front of me, *Madame*?" he offers.

I look past him at the next person waiting.

"Unless he's changed drastically in the last ten minutes, that is not my husband," I laugh.

The checkout girl picks up a plastic gun lying on the conveyor belt and holds it up to scan it.

"That's not mine," I say hastily.

"Is it yours?" she asks the man behind me.

"*Pardon*?" responds a familiar voice. Dennis has returned at last.

"No," I intercept, seeing Dennis' confusion. " I think it belongs to that woman with the toddler who went through before me." I point to the back of the customer and call out to her. "Is this your child's toy?"

She turns and accepts it gratefully.

"Are these yours, too, *Madame*?" The checkout girl is holding up a set of keys – *my keys* – and looking at the other woman.

"No," I say hurriedly. "They're mine. I put them down without thinking."

People are laughing. I find myself joining in and the checkout girl starts to giggle.

"It's so good to laugh," she says. "People usually glare, stare, or demand things and get annoyed. Here we have a happy queue! Thank you. You've made my day."

On the homeward bus I explain to Dennis what was happening.

"See?" I tell him. Not all French shop assistants are cross or miserable."

He smiles.

"Nevertheless," he says, "We're in one of the world's greatest cities and so far I've seen nothing but the inside of shops."

Right, I decide. You wait till tomorrow. But I simply grin in reply.

Chapter *Douze*

For the past five days Dennis and I have been doing everything in true tourist style. We've taken the funicular railway up the steep slope of *Montmartre* and photographed the breathtaking vista of Paris spread out below, admired the splendour of the domed basilica of *Sacré-Coeur*, strolled among the artists at work in nearby *Place du Tertre*, revelled in the architectural beauty and magnificent rose window for which the cathedral of *Notre Dame* is renowned and stood transfixed by the monumental iron structure that is the Eiffel Tower. We've walked our feet off exploring the streets of Paris. Then, over a late supper each evening, we've bored Nikki rigid with our impressions of the day's events, before hoisting our aching bodies up to our bed in the air, which is a bit steadier now that Dennis has tightened the bolts of its metal frame with an Allen key.

This morning we're ready to set off for the *Arc de Triomphe*. We had hoped to visit the *Louvre* but it doesn't look like we're going to have time so it will be a strong inducement for Dennis to come out again soon. Just let him *dare* grumble that he hasn't seen many Parisian highlights by the end of his week-long stay!

"Hang on a moment, Dennis. I must use the loo before we go. I don't know when I'll get another chance."

"In that case, better have two while you're at it," he calls out. "You might hold out a bit longer." Do I detect a touch of sarcasm?

It takes little more than half an hour to reach the heart of the city. I know this because Dennis times every journey obsessively. I've noticed he's taken a particular liking to the Paris Métro, which has given me an idea that I'll put to him later…

Coming out of the station of *Charles de Gaulle Etoile*, we face the island where Napoleon's spectacularly designed triumphal arch dominates one end of the world-famous *Avenue des Champs-Elysées*. We're not about to dice with death by attempting to cross the many lanes of traffic circling it. Dennis has concluded that French drivers are out to get him, even at quieter road junctions, so he's certainly not giving them their golden opportunity here. And for once I'm not arguing!

"Let's try those steps," he suggests. "There must be an underpass somewhere. Otherwise the road would be littered with bodies."

He's guessed correctly. It leads under the road past an exit to the island, where there's a long queue for tickets to climb the arch, from whose top there's said to be a stupendous view. Dennis is quite happy to believe this without experiencing it directly so we continue on, surfacing into daylight on the opposite side.

On the top step is one of Paris' numerous beggars. She sits, head bowed with her hand stretched out in supplication. Her "*Merci*" as I drop few coins into a cardboard box in front of her, is practically inaudible. The flap of the box has writing on it: "*J'ai faim. J'ai trois enfants et je n'ai pas de travail.*"

"She's hungry, has three children and no

work," I translate for Dennis.

Her shabby clothes contrast sharply with well-dressed passers-by wrapped up in their own affairs, most ignoring her completely A few paces further a Cartier shop, its window displaying expensive, opulent jewellery mocks her poverty-stricken state.

I feel so angry, so guilty that I'm part of a world that allows such inequality…

Ahead of us stretches the broad avenue of the *Champs-Elysées*, lined with trees whose colourful leaves are a reminder that autumn is well established. The road is bordered with spacious pavements, famous-named shops and cafés with tables neatly set outdoors. People sit, chat and read their newspapers, unruffled by the shadowy presence of an occasional beggar passing among them. One avenue, two worlds…

"Come on."Dennis senses my mood. "Let's have a coffee." He takes my hand and we wander on.

"This'll do," Dennis says and we go inside a small, comfortable café, reasonably priced for this area.

"I fancy a tart," he says with a wink.

I spread out a Métro map on the table.

"Close your eyes, Dennis and put your finger somewhere on the map. Then we'll see where we're going this afternoon."

"What do you mean?"

"We've seen plenty of tourist attractions. Let's now see the real Paris. I can't think of a better way than choosing a station at random."

"Fair enough." He shuts his eyes and stabs a

finger down on the map. "There!"

"We're going to…" I peer closely. "*Grands Boulevards*."

"Sounds interesting," he says.

We take time to enjoy our coffee and pastries.

On our descent into the Métro, we're intrigued by the strains of classical music filling the air, giving an ethereal note to this underworld.

"That's nice," Dennis says. "Where's it coming from?"

Following a bend in the passageway, we discover the answer – a small string orchestra is giving an impromptu concert for anyone who cares to listen and perhaps give a donation or buy one of their CDs displayed in a violin case. These musicians are clearly neither amateurs nor beggars.

An old woman, a carrier bag clutched in one hand, is using the other hand to beat time to their Vivaldi concerto, almost dancing with sheer pleasure.

We lean against the wall alongside other unhurried, music-loving travellers who've also paused for this entertainment, all the more splendid for being unexpected. Others hurry past, too intent on reaching their destinations.

The audience claps as the final chords combine with the rumbling echo of trains.

The orchestra launches into an animated arrangement of tunes from Bizet's *Carmen*. To our left three would-be divas, clearly familiar with the opera, join in with more confidence and gusto than genuine talent.

How strange, I reflect, that these brilliant

musicians are performing in a Métro station. And this venue has a powerful, reverberant acoustic that completely surrounds you, totally immersing you in the experience.

Dennis and I listen spellbound for a good twenty minutes as the group plays several more pieces, before we manage to pull ourselves away. Fortunately, I share his intense passion for the classics. The non-stop music in our house would otherwise have long since been a recipe for divorce.

"This is one of the exciting things about Paris," I tell Dennis. "Nearly everywhere you go, you come across something interesting."

We reach the platform and board the waiting train, which for a change is half empty. We sit opposite a young teenage lad. Glancing down, I'm astonished to catch sight of the life-sized head of a turkey poking out of the top of a shopping bag between his legs.

"That can't be real, can it?" I whisper to Dennis, whose gaze is also fixated on the turkey. "Do you think it's made of rubber?"

"No, it's alive," he whispers back. "If you watch, you'll see it move."

And sure enough, on closer inspection I notice its tiny alert, darting eyes and the quick, jerky movements of its head. Oddly, none of the other passengers is showing any interest. It's like this sort of thing is commonplace.

I can't resist making a comment.

"Is that your supper?" I ask, leaning forward with a grin.

The boy's eyes widen in shock and he shakes

his curly head vigorously.

"No, it's my pet."

My little joke has completely missed its mark. He looks quite offended.

I have seen notices on public transport stating that animals are permitted to accompany their owners in baskets or bags. To date, I've seen cats and miniature dogs but never a turkey.

Grands Boulevards certainly lives up to its name, with wide roads and expansive pavements.

Almost immediately we come upon a narrow arcade covered by an arched glass roof. It's lined with restaurants and small shops, many of which cater for collectors of everything from stamps to jewellery. We dawdle from window to window, fascinated by the range of unusual goods on offer.

We pause outside a smart bar selling draught cider – not the tipple we generally associate with the French.

"Do you want to try it?" I suggest.

"Great idea," Dennis replies, sitting at one of the tables.

A waiter comes out and we order.

The cider is cold, strong, delicious and surprisingly cheap.

Leaving this passage, we rejoin the main street and notice another entrance on the opposite side. We cross the road the easy way – using the Métro as an underpass.

This arcade, with its magnificently tiled floor is longer, lighter and grander than the one we've just left,. I'm particularly drawn to a window display of doll's houses, their rooms fully furnished in miniature, perfect to the last detail. It awakens the child within me. I'm years back in time, moving tiny figures and pieces of furniture, content in my own magical world of make-believe.

"Let's move on." Dennis' voice breaks the spell.

We return to the main street to explore further.

Large fashionable stores and chic boutiques give this part of the city an air of prosperity, again at odds with the sad, resigned faces of beggars. I'm upset by this divide. Giving a few coins might salve my conscience for the moment but it does nothing to solve their problem.

I remain pensive on the journey home. I wish I could make the world a more caring place.

Chapter *Treize*

I've been psyching myself up to make this call. Breathing deeply, I dial Nikki's number.

"Hi Mum." Her voice sounds strained.

"Are you ok, Nikki?"

"Yes thanks, never felt better. How about you and Dad?"

The forced lightness of her tone doesn't fool me. But I ignore it, not wanting to behave like a fussy mother.

"We're fine. Actually, I'm ringing to let you know that we're planning a visit to the apartment at the end of the month. We'd like to see Paris in the springtime."

There's silence at the other end of the line. Has she rung off?

"Nikki?"

"Yes, I'm still here. But no, you can't come then."

"Look Nikki, I'm getting really fed up with this. Ever since we left in October you've stalled every time I've mentioned us coming out."

"Well, I'm sorry, Mum. It's simply not convenient."

"Why not?" I feel intensely irritated.

"Because it isn't. You'll have to take my word for it. I'll explain when I see you."

"What's the mystery, Nikki? And when will we see you?"

"It won't be long, I promise," she says curtly.

"I'm hoping to move out soon. I've been offered a chance to rent an apartment in the heart of the city. In fact, I'm going to look at it on Friday. It'll be much nicer for you and Dad to have this place to yourselves. After all, it is your apartment."

I don't bother to mention that it seems to me she's already assumed ownership of it.

"Nikki, don't do that. You know you can't afford it."

"Look, it's my life, Mum. And besides, I'd be getting an incredibly good deal through a friend. I must run. Talk to you later. Love to you and Dad."

The line goes dead.

I know something's wrong but I can't pin it down. My imagination is spinning out of control, envisaging one catastrophic possibility after another…

Perhaps she's knocked a tin of that nightmarish blue paint she was intending to use on her wall over the floor instead…

Have some of her friends trashed the place during a wild party and it's taking months to put things right…?

Or worse, have squatters moved in while she was at work, leaving her homeless? Come to think of it, she never did get that landline installed and whenever we've chatted recently I'm sure I've heard street noises in the background. And from what I've been told, squatters are a common problem in Paris and getting rid of them is a long-term project…

"Trouble?" My friend Fran looks up at me over her coffee cup. "You've gone quite pale."

"It's Nikki. She keeps blocking us from visiting our apartment. But she won't tell me why."

"I shouldn't worry," Fran reassures me. "You know what kids are like. She's probably asserting her independence and doesn't want anyone to spoil it, especially the parents."

"No, it's more than that. I sense that she's sort of … tense and distracted. Still, she says she's hoping to rent somewhere in the centre of Paris soon so we'll be able to go out then. I do hope everything is the way we left it."

"You'll be lucky. But don't forget it's not that long since your breakdown and you're probably a bit over-sensitive."

"Maybe you're right. I'm probably being over-protective and there's nothing whatsoever to worry about."

"So, when are you going to take me to your flat? I bet you could do with my help to personalise it. And I've never seen Paris. Could be good for both of us."

Thinking about the superb job she's done on her own bungalow, I have to admit that this could be an ideal opportunity to benefit from her practical skills and give her a holiday at the same time.

"Tell, you what, Fran, when she moves out, I'll take you up on that."

*

"Hey, Mum!" Nikki sounds buoyant.

"Yes, Nikki," I say, relieved but guarded, knowing from experience that her tone could mean anything from a change of boyfriend or her job to winning the French Lottery.

"You know that apartment I told you I was going to check out?" She continues without waiting for a reply. "Well, it's not far from Gare du Nord, in a really lively street and because one of my friends knows the landlord I can get it for a knock-down rent. So I'm moving in the first week of June when the present tenant leaves. And before you say anything I'm going to thoroughly spring-clean this apartment, ready for you both."

Taken aback by the exuberance of her lengthy outburst, I don't answer immediately.

"Are you there, Mum?"

"Yes, Nikki, and I'm pleased for you but are you sure it's a wise decision?"

"Absolutely. I'd be daft to pass up an opportunity like this. You'd normally have to pay double the rent in that area."

"Perhaps the knock-down price reflects a knock-down building." I'm only half joking.

"Oh, ha, ha! Actually, it's perfect – just what I wanted."

"Well, good luck with it. And keep in touch," I add quickly, before she rings off.

I dial Fran's number.

"Guess what," I tell her. "Nikki's leaving the flat at the beginning of June. Were you serious about coming to Paris with me?"

"Too right, I was. I'm ready whenever you are."

"Great. How about we go for a month in July, after Dennis and I return from Italy? He can fend for himself for a while. I'll book the tickets the moment I know Nikki's actually left."

*

The suitcase is almost full. I'm selecting and rejecting clothes for our imminent holiday.

I'm looking forward to seeing Venice again. The awesome sight of St Marks from the ferry always makes as great an impact as it did the first time. And the campsite where we stay on the edge of the Adriatic has its own unique magical atmosphere. What's more, Dennis, who normally regards holidays as an unnecessary evil, gets as much caught up in the entire experience as I do.

The phone's insistent ringing interrupts my reverie. A sixth sense tells me it's Nikki.

"Hi, Mum!"

My stomach tenses. How is it that after just two words I already know that this isn't simply a social call?

I get straight to the point. "What's the matter, Nikki?"

"Don't panic, Mum, it's nothing much. But I thought you should know that when I moved out of your apartment I left the keys with the agent so that you can pick them up when you arrive. That way you're not dependent on me getting them to you. And I gave her my mobile number in case there was ever a problem."

What agent? Ah yes, I know. She's talking about the woman who handles the affairs of the whole apartment building.

"Is there a problem then?"

"Not now. But she contacted me a few days

ago to say that the grocer in the shop below rang her to report water coming down the outside of your kitchen wall and rang her."

"Oh no!" I exclaim.

"Mum, listen. It's not serious. The agent gave a plumber your keys. He's repaired a leak in the main water pipe that runs through the block and you don't have to pay anything. It comes out of the general fund."

I'm not sure what she means but I'll have to take her word for it.

"The trouble was, the day after the plumber came the grocer noticed your window had been left open…"

"Tell me the worst," I say quickly, increasingly certain that squatters have climbed into the apartment and taken up residence.

"He called the agent again," she continues, "and she's been in and closed it. The grocer told me when I collected my post this morning. So everything's ok, Mum, and you can calm down."

How can she detect panic from my silence? I release the breath I've been holding.

"Are you sure there are no squatters?"

"What on earth are you talking about?" Her genuine puzzlement is all the reassurance I need.

"Never mind, Nikki. Thanks for keeping me informed. By the way, how is the new apartment?"

"Fantastic. I can't wait to show you it. I've managed to get most of the things I need for it from the pavement. That's where people dump things they don't want."

So my daughter's furnished her apartment with

stuff that was destined for the rubbish tip. I can't begin to imagine what it looks like. Is she penniless or enterprising? I'm torn between pity and admiration. I daren't voice my thoughts.

"You won't believe the kind of things I've found. A lot of it's in such good condition that you wonder why they've thrown it out."

"Maybe some of it was waiting to be collected by an owner."

"No, it was definitely unwanted."

I don't see how she can know this, but I let it pass.

"Marcel's here. He says *bonjour*."

"Same to him. Take care now. Love you."

I return to my packing, remembering the bedside table I made out of a wooden orange box as a child. Has Nikki inherited my quirky creativity?

*

Dennis and I are lazing in the hot sun, half dozing on the grass outside our tent in the peacefulness of an Italian siesta. I'm listening to the distant, muffled rumble of the waves and faint cries of seagulls circling overhead. I can't remember when I last experienced such blissfully warm, comfortable contentment. I'm at one with myself and the world around me.

My mobile vibrates fiercely in my pocket, stirring me into reluctant wakefulness.

Who's so rudely intruding on my restful state?

"Yes?" I answer brusquely.

"Hi, Mum." It had to be Nikki, didn't it? With

her telepathic instinct she invariably homes in on precisely the wrong moment.

"Yes, Nikki, what is it?" I don't hide my annoyance.

"Are you enjoying your holiday, Mum?"

"I was till you woke me. Did you phone just to ask me that?"

"No, sorry. I didn't mean to disturb you. I'll be quick. I've got some good news and bad news. Which do you want first?"

My stomach somersaults as my mind leaps to one conclusion: she's pregnant!

"Give me the bad news," I say tensely.

"Are you sitting down?"

"Nikki, get on with it! What's happened?"

"The nasty bit is that your apartment is full of water…"

"WHAT…!" I explode.

"Let me finish. The great part is that the buildings insurance that's included in your quarterly charges will cover it and you'll end up with a brand new place."

I've run out of words.

"The agent rang," she continues, my silence clearly conveying my temporary loss of coherent speech. "She told me that the main water pipe, which was repaired last month, sprang another leak. And when it rained on the squatters on the floor below yours, they called the fire brigade, who smashed your kitchen window to get in and managed to stem the flow till the agent sent in a plumber. It's lucky I'd left my keys with her. I don't know all the details but don't worry, she's also getting a glazier to replace your window."

"DON'T WORRY?" I screech, ignoring the alarmed faces of neighbouring holidaymakers.

"Mum, please stop shouting! Everything's under control. It's in good hands."

Yes, but *whose* hands?

Forcing myself to behave as near-normally as I can under the circumstances I lower my voice.

"But I can't get out there till next month. I booked for Fran and me to come over in July."

"That will be time enough to fill out insurance papers. I've notified your insurance company and the agent knows your situation because I've explained it to her. Even if you were here now, there'd be nothing you could do. Your apartment has to dry out before it can be sorted."

"Ok. Well, thanks for letting me know," I say, trying to resign myself to the inevitable.

"Enjoy the rest of your holiday. It'll all work out well in the end. Bye, Mum."

I replace the phone in my pocket. So much for my siesta.

"Dennis, wake up! Something awful's happened!"

He blinks rapidly. "What have you done now?"

"It's not me, it's the apartment! It's been flooded!"

"Not possible. It's in mid-air on top of a hill," he comments lazily. "And as far as I know, they're having a heat wave in France."

"How can you be so flippant? That pipe in the kitchen's leaked again. Nikki rang me a few moments ago."

"We're insured, aren't we?"

"Yes but…"

"Well there you are, then." He closes his eyes again, leaving me fretting and envious of his ability to switch off. I know this will nag at the back of my head until I'm able to assess the damage for myself and can see that something's being done about it.

Chapter *Quatorze*

I can see my Nikki waving eagerly amid the waiting throng at the exit from the Eurostar platform. We haven't seen each other since her Christmas visit to England nearly seven months ago. Fran and I weave in and out of the mass exodus of passengers towards her as fast as our suitcases allow.

I hug her close, then draw back, cupping her face in my hands.

"It's marvellous to see you again," I enthuse." I'd almost forgotten what you looked like."

She smiles happily and embraces us both.

"Let's get your Orange Travel Cards," she urges.

Fran hands her the small photo she's brought for the purpose and we traipse after Nikki to the Métro ticket office.

It's a struggle to manoeuvre our cases through the turnstiles, which were surely designed to permit the passage of human beings *minus* their bulky baggage – strange, considering that the Gare du Nord is a gateway to and from much of France and Europe.

We get to the platform in the nick of time. The warning tone signalling imminent closure of the train doors causes us to dash towards the nearest compartment, which is filling rapidly.

A teenage girl suddenly appears beside Fran, smiles at her, helps her into the train with her case and steps back onto the platform. I hear Fran yell and see another girl reaching through the closing doors, trying to wrench Fran's bag from around her waist. But she's forced to pull back as the automatic doors slam shut.

"What cheek!" Fran exclaims. "Did you see that?"

I nod, unable to speak. I'm more shaken than Fran looks.

"I saw it coming, Fran," Nikki tells her. "But I couldn't react fast enough. If we'd arrived a few seconds earlier she'd have got away with it. Thieves often do this kind of thing on the Métro, especially in tourist areas. I should have mentioned it. They hang around on platforms and while one distracts you, the other catches you off guard. I've seen it happen before."

I glance around continually, clutching my handbag tightly to me. Nikki is watching me with mild amusement.

"Don't get paranoid, Mum. Take sensible precautions and you'll be fine. You won't enjoy your stay if you're living in fear. This can happen in any city anywhere."

Wise words indeed! She's right. But it doesn't stop me feeling wary.

Coming up the escalator, we pause to bask briefly in the glorious warmth of a Parisian summer before wending our way uphill.

Fran and I trudge up the stairs to the apartment with our luggage. My suitcase didn't feel this heavy when I set off this morning!

Nikki's gone ahead with my keys to unlock for us.

I hear an odd scraping noise from above.

Sweating profusely, I summon every ounce of

energy for the final flight of stairs. At the top, Nikki's face confirms my worst fears.

"Remember, Mum, in a couple of months it won't look anything like it does now."

Her comment fails to reassure me.

Standing at the doorway I'm horrified, totally unprepared for the devastation – grossly warped floorboards with deep gouges where the front door had to be pushed open forcibly, heavily-stained, watermarked walls and swollen skirting boards.

I cannot conceal my distress.

"Welcome to my little flat, Fran," I say unhappily, the tears pouring down my cheeks.

*

Nikki made a concentrated effort last night to lift my spirits with a bottle of wine and a tasty takeaway and Fran was on top form with her quirky sense of humour. But it took me hours to muster sufficient emotional strength to think more positively about the state of my treasured apartment.

I was somewhat consoled that, surprisingly, it didn't smell musty, even before we opened the windows. And fortunately, the damp hasn't affected any furniture or bedding. I naively assumed they'd be dry anyway; it never occurred to me that we might not have been able to stay a night, let alone a month, in an apartment that had been completely flooded. Someone, somewhere, must be looking after me.

I'm determined to maintain the upbeat mood I got up in this morning. Fran was delighted with the

Continental breakfast I bought and served up and we're about to carry out a closer inspection of the damage to review what improvements she can make in these circumstances.

As usual, Fran is her organised self with tape measure and pen and paper, ready to list everything I'll need to buy.

We're standing in what was Nikki's room, now temporarily Fran's bedroom.

"I'm going to turn this into a lounge, or *salon* as the French call it," I inform her.

"You're lucky in here because the walls aren't wet so I can paint them. What colour do you want?"

I think for a moment. "I'd love pale green. Oh, and a corner shelf to hold a lamp would look good over by the window."

Fran begins measuring the room.

"Did you hear a tap on the door?" I ask her.

"No. I think you've got water on the brain."

I flash her a wry smile. Looking through the spyhole I see the distorted image of a bespectacled young man.

"*C'est qui*?" I call.

"Your next door neighbour, Madame," he answers.

Curious, I open the door a fraction.

"*Bonjour*," he says, smiling broadly.

I drag the resisting door inwards and shake his outstretched hand.

"I heard voices so I thought I'd introduce myself. I'm Olivier. And you are…?"

"Polly. Pleased to meet you. I'm here with my

friend Fran. Would you like to come in for a coffee?"

He accepts my invitation and follows me into the lounge, where he greets Fran cordially. He has the sort of face that looks ready to burst into laughter at any second. She smiles at him but unable to speak French, is silent for a change.

She excuses herself to make coffee.

"It's terrible what happened here." Olivier is shaking his head solemnly.

"You heard about it then?" I say.

"Yes, I was in my apartment the day the firemen came. I'm decorating it for my fiancée. We're getting married next year."

"Congratulations."

"Thank you. Anyway, as I said, I was busy painting the windowsill when a ladder appeared on the outside of the window. Then a fireman climbed up and started banging on the glass, commanding me to open up. He said I had a problem with water pouring from my apartment into the one beneath. I shouted back that I was working here and would have noticed if anything was wrong. But he insisted that if I didn't let him in he would have to break the glass. Of course, I didn't want him to smash my window so I told him I'd unlock the door."

Fran brings in mugs of coffee. Olivier pauses to stir three teaspoons of sugar into his, before continuing.

"Two firemen looked around and could see for themselves that everything was in order. I told them the water must have been coming from your apartment. So because it was empty they broke in through your kitchen window where one of them told me afterwards they had to turn off a tap that usually connects to a washing machine. He said someone had turned it on and just left it. Naturally, your apartment filled up with water before it seeped through the ceiling onto the squatters that live below and they called the emergency service."

I'm dumbfounded.

"Can you show me which tap you're talking about?"

We go in to the kitchen, where he points to a small blue tap hidden away beside the sink unit. I'd never noticed it before.

Whoever could have left it on? It must have been that plumber the agent sent in to fix the leaky pipe. He was dippy enough to leave the window open.

I thank Olivier who returns to gulp down his coffee and looks at his watch.

"I must go now," he says. "I have a lot to do today. I hope to see you again soon."

Bidding him *au revoir* I close the door behind him.

I repeat the gist of our conversation to Fran.

"That agent got it wrong," I add. "She claimed that the problem was a burst water pipe, not a gushing tap. Either she was given false information or she was protecting her plumber."

"Getting a backhander from him, most likely," Fran comments cynically. "Do you realise, Polly, that water has been an important theme in your life recently?"

"What do you mean?"

"Well, when you moved in you had no running water. So your guardian angel, who obviously has a dry sense of humour, decided to give you more than you'd bargained for. Maybe someone Up There's having a laugh at your expense."

"Very funny, Fran! Talking of water, I need the loo."

Chapter *Quinze*

I've spent several days showing Fran some tourist landmarks and making regular forays with her to *Leroy Merlin* and the local shops to buy everything she needs to personalise my apartment. – everything except wood to make shelving. Aside from the fact that it's expensive, Fran reckoned that if Nikki could furnish her rooms with oddments folk don't want, we should be able to find some discarded wooden furniture she can cannibalise. We scoured the neighbourhood but without success, finding nothing but mattresses and televisions – rather useless as potential shelves! However, by pure luck, when we borrowed a cellar key from the grocer to explore the dank-smelling recesses of the cave-like area beneath the building, we happened upon some melamine planks, which, judging by the layers of dust that have settled on them, must have been there for years. Perfect!

As Fran prefers to work alone with just the radio for company (she doesn't care what comes out of it as long as it provides a background noise), I'm off to the launderette to replenish our dwindling supply of clean clothes.

"See you later," I call. "Don't bother to see me out."

"Wasn't going to," she retorts. "I'm going to start the painting. Oh, and by the way, this drill's stopped working work."

"Have you tried plugging it in?" I ask, returning to see for myself.

"I'm not as stupid as I look, you know."

She's quite right. It's completely dead.

"I'll take it back later. Bye."

I amble into town, my shopping trolley bouncing on the uneven paving slabs, content to enjoy the morning sun on my skin. This promises to be another scorching day.

In the pedestrian precinct I window-shop idly. An ambulance, its lights flashing, overtakes me and brakes to an abrupt halt. I hope it's not for me. Does someone know something I don't…?

Two paramedics leap out and sprint into a *Quick* restaurant. In my usual nosey fashion, I'm curious to see what the emergency is. Perhaps somebody has choked on a burger, slipped on a wet floor or collapsed with food poisoning…

With my nose pressed to the window I watch as they approach the counter. One of them points upwards to the illuminated menu. They speak to an assistant, collect takeaways, run back and jump into the ambulance, which reverses into a side street.

Phew! Now that's what I call fast food!

Shaking my head in disbelief I continue on to the laundrette. I push the door open, then freeze. The ear-piercing wail of a siren rises in a painful crescendo. What's going on? I look around me. People are continuing to shop, chat, or stroll without looking remotely perturbed by what to me is a worryingly dramatic interruption to everyday life.

Inside the laundrette I approach a middle-aged man, seated watching his washing tumbling in the machine.

"Please could you tell me what that noise is?"

As he opens his mouth to speak, the siren

ceases.

"It's the nuclear air raid alert."

I haven't heard the news recently. Perhaps there's a war on…

"Are we going to be blown to pieces?" I ask, surprised at his calmness. "Because if we are, I'm not going to waste time or money washing clothes."

He grins.

"It's not a problem, Madame. This is a regular test on the first Wednesday of the month."

"Then this would be a good time to drop a bomb on Paris, if everyone is used to hearing and ignoring it. But if it were a genuine attack I presume the siren would continue."

"I imagine so," he agrees.

I thank him and try to work out how to follow the complicated instructions to wash and dry laundry. He must have noticed my puzzlement as he proffers his help. He guides me patiently through procedures that would probably have outwitted me.

We chat during the hour and a half it takes to complete the process. I learn that his name is Jean-Paul, that an accident left him with a permanently injured back, obliging him to give up his job as a TV studio technician and that he's staying with a friend after a water pipe burst in his own apartment. Is there a French epidemic of burst pipes?

I relate the complex story of my own leak. I tell him that being English, I don't know how, or even if, insurance works in France.

He compliments me on my French and says he's well placed to give advice, having grappled with insurance companies in the past.

"You need to know that it's essential to maintain pressure on them, otherwise nothing will happen."

He's easy to converse with. I understand each point he makes because he speaks clearly and reasonably slowly and by the time I've folded my dry clothes he's offered to have a look at the broken drill I've mentioned.

I can't ignore the nagging uncertainty about taking a relative stranger back to the apartment. But there's no time to consider it as he's decided to accompany me up the hill.

I introduce Fran to Jean-Paul.

"She doesn't speak French," I say, by way of excuse for my paint-spattered friend who looks idiotic, poised statue-like and open-mouthed with a dripping brush in her upraised hand.

I pass him the drill. Within seconds it vibrates into action.

"It's faulty. The switch works intermittently," he explains.

Turning down my offer of a coffee he says he's happy to have been of assistance but must now rush off for an important rendezvous.

As I close the door behind him, Fran explodes at me.

"You can't just invite total strangers back like that! Wherever did you pick *him* up? For all you knew, he could have been an axe murderer!"

I'm reprieved by my phone ringing.

"Can we meet up in half an hour?" Nikki's tone is insistent. "Just you and me. I've got the afternoon off and there's something I need to talk to you about."

We arrange a place to meet. I'm bewildered. What could be so urgent?

"There's food in the fridge, Fran. Must go. Nikki wants to see me immediately. I'll explain later."

Without giving her a chance to respond I'm out of the door.

Hurrying back to town, I'm becoming overwhelmed with anxiety. The high-speed washing machine of my mind is spinning thoughts around randomly. Has Nikki lost her job? Has she been evicted? Is she in trouble?

Nikki is waiting for me outside the bar. Something's amiss. Where's her usual sparkle?

We sit at a table in the open air, the afternoon heat contradicting the chill inside me. I remain silent. She'll speak in her own time. You can't rush Nikki.

"How about a strawberry kir, Mum?"

"What's in it?"

"White wine with strawberry cordial. It's quite sweet."

"I'd like that. I'll get them."

I signal to a waiter who comes across and takes our order.

"What did you want to discuss with me?" I ask Nikki, unable to hold out any longer.

"I'll get round to that in a while. I wasn't actually planning to *discuss* anything. I simply need to tell you something. Let's have our drinks first."

By the third round I'm slightly tipsy and practically bursting with impatience. Nearly two hours have passed. We've talked about her job, her apartment, her social life, the usefulness of my new French phone…

And she hasn't yet touched on the reason for our meeting. My train of thought is running out of steam…

"Nikki, please stop stalling. You had something important to tell me. Why are you being so cagey?"

"It's not that easy."

I lean forward, waiting.

Nikki sighs. "I've got a confession to make," she blurts out.

My stomach becomes a food blender on the highest setting.

She continues. "I'd never run a place before. When I was living in your apartment I found it terribly difficult to make ends meet. I had to come up with a plan quickly because my bank was threatening to close my account."

She hesitates, watching my face. I've already decided that she must somehow have succeeded in selling the apartment in my absence to pay off enormous debts.

"Go on," I say, flatly, fearful that it's a fait accompli and she's about to name the date when the new owner moves in.

"I decided to sublet yours and Dad's room to my friends."

"You did WHAT?" I'm incredulous.

"Let me finish. It worked fine for a few

months. But then when you kept saying you wanted to come over, I couldn't be sure you wouldn't turn up out of the blue. I knew I had to get rid of them fast so I told them to leave."

"And did they?"

"No. That was the problem. They said they would but did nothing about it. Finally I got desperate and arranged for Annette to ring, speaking English, and pretend she was you. I made sure they could overhear by switching my mobile to speakerphone and standing in the hallway. After the phoney call I told them that you insisted on coming to the apartment the following week. They left the next day, regarding you as a fate worse than death!"

"Thanks a lot! But I've glad you've told me." I don't tell her that, compared with the disastrous scenario I'd created, this is almost comical.

"Did they return their keys?"

She nods.

"All the same, I'll feel more secure if I get an extra strong lock fitted tomorrow. They might have had another set cut."

"Your apartment will probably be unique with four locks," she says with a half smile.

We hug each other goodbye. Nikki looks distinctly lighter since she shared her secret. And a hefty weight's been lifted from me.

Time to face Fran.

Chapter *Seize*

Between us we've accomplished a considerable amount. The palest green walls with deep green skirting boards and melamine shelving have enhanced the cosy ambience of the salon, while shelves in our bedroom and the kitchen have created some storage space. Even the shower room door now closes and locks. Fran has done a fantastic job, using tools we bought here and the ones she brought with her. I've added a carpet and numerous little embellishments to further personalise the apartment and turned my humble toilet window into a stained glass creation worthy of *Notre Dame*, using a sheet of multicoloured, self-adhesive frosted plastic. Now I'm no longer overlooked.

Armed with Jean-Paul's warning, I eventually plucked up sufficient courage to tackle my French insurance agent. I've been to the office several times to find out what's happening, which, on the whole, is not a lot yet. What has become noticeable, however, is the way the staff cringe as I walk in, whilst still addressing me with formal politeness.

The agent explained company procedures (which involve a great deal of paperwork) and assured me that initially they would arrange for their Expert to do a survey of the damage next month and write a report. She pronounced the word Expert with an importance that suggested the need for a capital letter. The French for "Expert" turns out to be *Expert*. The agent promised to phone and let me know the date of his visit.

These lengthy conversations served a triple purpose: it kept me from under Fran's feet, informed me about how insurance works over here and enabled me to achieve a consistent fluency in French.

*

The rest of our stay has been taken up with numerous outings to the famous *Place du Tertre* in *Montmartre*, where we've stood for hours, admiring and talking with artists using pastel, oil and watercolours to magnificent effect. I was particularly drawn to, if not by, a few who've been working there for thirty-odd years, producing remarkably lifelike portraits of tourists.

Days have flown by. And with only one more before our return to England I have two important tasks left. This morning I'm going to *Leroy Merlin* to get a refund for the drill, which Fran has finished with and I don't need, especially with its intermittently working switch, and this afternoon I have an appointment with an estate agent.

"See you lunchtime. My bus is due in two minutes," I inform Fran, who's busy making blue drapes for the salon window to match the sofa bed. I run down the stairs and across the road, for once without popping into the local bar to drink coffee and chat with Martine, who's always so pleased to see us.

The bus pulls up as I arrive and I squeeze in breathlessly.

"Move further down the bus," the driver calls

out, glancing in his rear-view mirror. Can't he see that a token sway is the most anyone can manage?

Abruptly an uncomfortably loud, continuous warbling pierces the air like a concentrated flock of starlings. Faces above, around and below me react with alarm. It takes a moment or two before it registers that the tiny, personal warning device round my neck has been knocked from its pin and fallen to the floor, setting it off. With difficulty I retrieve it from between the skirted and trousered legs surrounding me, and reattach it, muttering *"Pardon"* repeatedly during the silence that follows.

My face is burning. I've become the focus of the French equivalent of "tut-tutting".

Two stops further on the bus empties half its load on the edge of a large high-rise council estate.

I stagger to a seat to recover.

The official notice on the window beside me catches my attention:

'You may open or close the windows as you wish. In the case of a dispute between passengers, priority is given to the one who wants the window closed.'

Must remember that!

My amusement breaks the tension inside me.

Standing nervously in the queue at Customer Services in *Leroy Merlin* apprehension is building again. I don't intend mentioning the faulty switch. It would complicate matters – I want a refund, not a replacement. I've heard that getting your money back in French shops is generally difficult if not impossible. Yet on the wall a poster states categorically that, should a customer change their mind for whatever reason, provided the item is returned in its original packaging with the appropriate receipt within a month of purchase, a full refund will be given. Where's the catch?

It appears from the argument taking place in front of me that you have to follow the instructions to the letter. The assistant is insisting that because the Stanley knife packaging is damaged, nothing can be done.

The customer shrieks, "I don't want a refund, I want a replacement!" She's waving the knife around furiously. I keep my distance.

The assistant confers with two others and makes a phone call, while the queue lengthens steadily.

She sighs. "In this instance, Madame, we will replace it. However, this is highly irregular."

It's my turn.

Steeling myself I launch into my prepared and much rehearsed speech.

"My daughter bought me a drill for my birthday so I won't be needing this one."

The assistant unsmilingly scrutinises my face and my box as I speak. I hope she doesn't have a concealed lie detector.

Without a word, she takes my receipt, opens her till and hands me the money.

I walk out quickly before she changes her mind.

*

Fran looks worried.

"I don't know what's wrong with the boiler. I switched it on to heat up hours ago after we'd showered. But the water's cold."

Not this! Not now, when there's no time to get it fixed.

"I'll go and ask Martine if she knows a plumber."

I rush down to the bar.

"*Bonjour,* Martine. I have an emergency."

Her smile fades as she senses my panic. She closes her hands round mine.

"What is the matter, *ma chérie*?"

She listens patiently as I explain, using considerably more words than necessary.

"I know a retired plumber who's excellent. He often does jobs for me on the black. Give me your number, Polly, and I'll get him to call you."

I write it down for her and she disappears into a back room.

"He's not there," she says, re-emerging, "but I've left a message on his answerphone.

"I'm a plumber, Madame," a voice besides me croaks.

Turning, I see an old man leaning against the bar, grinning lopsidedly.

"Can you look at her boiler straight away, Pierre?" Martine asks him. "She lives a few doors down."

"Certainly," he obliges. "Lead on, Madame."

I cast Martine an anxious look. She winks at me.

"He's ok. I know him, he's a regular," she

assures me.

But out in the street, Pierre stumbles along the pavement and I begin to suspect he's had a drink too many. Best to be tactful.

"I don't want to take up your afternoon," I tell him.

"No, it's my pleasure." His crooked smile is not the reassurance I need.

I can't let him into the apartment. What would Fran say?

But attempts to deter him aren't working. He's bent on accompanying me. Pausing to steady himself with the help of the stair rail, he puffs and blows with every step.

Ignoring Fran, who's glowering at me in the hallway, disturbed no doubt by the slurred speech of our visitor, I show Pierre into the kitchen and point to the boiler.

"*Ah, oui!*" he exclaims, swaying gently.

"Who the heck's that?" Fran hisses in my ear.

"It's Pierre the plumber. Martine knows him," I hiss back.

"But he's pissed!"

"I didn't know that till the fresh air hit him."

"Who's next? Bob the Builder? Are you making a collection of weird Frenchmen?" she says, retreating to the salon.

Pierre raises a shaky hand to the wires overhead that connect the boiler to the electricity.

"Shall I turn off the power?" I suggest quickly.

"No, not worth it," he mumbles, pulling on the wires.

I feel in my pocket for my mobile, ready to call

the emergency services, though I'm not sure whether it's to protect my safety or his.

He requests a screwdriver.

I watch riveted as his bony fingers disconnect the wires. In slow motion, the index finger of his other hand moves towards the bare terminals.

I screw up my eyes, unable to move or speak, waiting, scared of what's about to happen…

Sparks fly between the wires and his finger and there's a distinct odour of burning flesh.

"*Merde!*" he says letting the wires drop and sucking his finger.

Unbelievably, he's upright, his cheeks haven't lost their ruddy colour and he's scratching his bald head.

"Ah!" He's obviously had another crazy thought.

"No, no, please leave it," I plead. "I've got to go out."

"You women are too impatient. It will take a while to repair. Give me a glass of wine."

"I'll make you a coffee. But no wine."

He shrugs philosophically. "Forget it. I'll do without."

I go to the salon, where Fran is sewing.

"I can't get rid of him. Would you mind terribly if I left him with you for about an hour?"

Before she can refuse, I explain the urgency of my meeting with the estate agent.

She doesn't look exactly happy.

"Go if you must. I can handle his sort if I have to."

"Thanks, Fran. I owe you one. I'll be as quick

as I can."

*

In the estate agent's office, a short, tubby man with a toothbrush moustache shakes my hand and gestures towards the seat facing him. He leans forward, his arms on his desk, hands folded, peering through bifocals over several piles of neatly stacked papers.

"What can I do for you, Madame?"

I reach into my bag and produce a weighty folder of documents.

"I'm thinking of selling my apartment soon," I say, looking at him directly. "But, being English and therefore a bit stupid, I need to check that I have the correct papers." What I don't tell him is that the real reason for my visit is that one of Nikki's friends, who looked at my paperwork, couldn't see the deeds so I'm concerned that I may not legally own the apartment. I have no intention whatsoever of selling my cosy nook.

He skims through the papers, verbally verifying each one to himself. Suddenly he frowns. What's he found – or failed to find?

"The price you paid was unbelievably low."

Confessing I was party to a *sous-la-table* transaction would probably not be in my best interests.

"I bought cheaply from a friend. It needed work doing on it." I say quickly. "And since then I've made a lot of improvements."

"Well, the Town Hall will no doubt question

this discrepancy. But I have an arrangement with them, so you needn't worry." He winks knowingly at me and rubs his hands together.

How many bureaucrats are involved in property scams, I wonder.

"Everything is in order, Madame," he pronounces. "When would you like us to come and quote on your apartment?"

"I'll be in touch next month," I reply breezily, reflecting that I've lied more this week than in the past ten years.

The world now looks a much better place.

As I open the door to my legally owned apartment, even the fact that Pierre has left without effecting a repair to the boiler does not fill me with dismay. At least he hasn't made the situation worse as far as I can tell.

Martine's proper plumber rings.

"Probably the thermostat," he concludes when I describe the symptoms. "I'll come by later."

*

The plumber has been and gone. Hot running water is restored. Fran and I have cleaned and tidied up and are off to celebrate our last evening in Paris at a typically French restaurant, a treat I shall miss when I'm back here with Dennis.

Chapter *Dix-Sept*

Having waited in vain until the end of August for an appointment with the Expert, I've decided it's time to come face-to-face with my insurance agent again. And, as Jean-Paul advised, it's probably the only way to get things moving.

Dennis is in holiday mood as he tucks into his usual brand of muesli, which he packed despite my protest that the French do sell perfectly edible food.

We sip our coffee, luxuriating in the comfort of our sun-filled salon.

Last night, though taken aback by extent of the water damage, Dennis was generous with his compliments about the work Fran and I put in, especially in this room.

"So where do you want to go today?" he asks.

"First I must visit the insurance. But after that, how about we go to the artists' quarter at *Montmartre*?"

"Whatever you like, love."

We stroll hand in hand to the agents'. Faces look up from behind their computer monitors as we enter the office, those nearest us nodding and uttering a curt '*bonjour'* before returning their work, except for my usual agent, who rises from her chair, hurries towards us smiling, and shakes our hands.

"Has the Expert contacted you?"

"No, no-one's written or phoned," I reply softly, not wishing to address the entire workforce.

"That's strange." She frowns. "I gave him your English number. I'll ring and ask him to send you a date."

While she's speaking, Dennis and I become intrigued by a poster on the wall behind her. It's a black and white photograph of a steam locomotive whose front end lies in a street, its rear propped high against a station wall through which it has obviously crashed. The caption below it informs us that this was a disaster that occurred at the *Gare Montparnasse* in Paris in 1895. Compared with the magnitude of that damage, what happened in my apartment was not so serious. But I still want it dealt with!

The agent interrupts my musings.

"He's not in his office right now. His secretary will ask him to write to you."

I thank her, she shakes our hands, wishes us good day and we leave to a chorus of '*au revoir*'.

On the train, an elderly busker is serenading travellers with his violin. I'm not sure whether he's begging or if this is his regular occupation. Is there a difference, I wonder, as he stops playing and tours the carriage to collect money. From what I can see it doesn't seem to pay well. He gets off at the next station and stays on the platform, presumably to await the next train.

Coming out of *Anvers* Métro station we pause to watch a group of breakdancers performing to rap music from a cd player, contorting their bodies into seemingly impossible shapes to rounds of enthusiastic applause from a crowd of tourists clutching cameras.

Across the road hordes of women are rummaging furiously through untidy piles of clothes heaped in boxes and on tables, in spaces where a normal shop would have windows. Dennis watches from a safe distance as, curious, I join the scrum taking place inside and out, like a massive jumble sale with people frantically scrabbling for the best bargain. These garments, though creased, are unused and a fraction of normal prices – jumpers, coats, trousers, blouses for all ages, sizes and sexes for a Euro or two. Prices reflect the shop's name, *Sympa*, meaning nice, but on the whole the quality is poor.

Tati, the shop opposite, equally crowded and also cheap, sells a random mixture of goods – tacky vases, babies' bottles, bed-linen, assorted dvds, clocks, men's shirts, underwear, cheap jewellery, high-quality German toilet rolls…

We climb the ancient cobbled street lined with open-fronted shops displaying miniature, cheap looking Eiffel towers and the like – Parisian souvenirs made in China for relatives to gush over and hide until your next reappearance. And judging by the swarms of people inside, business is booming.

"Tourists will buy anything," Dennis remarks caustically.

"I'm desperate for a toilet," I tell him. But his gaze is now focussed on the aesthetically pleasing splendour of the white dome of the *Sacré-Coeur* looming impressively on its hill above us against a vivid blue sky.

Intent on more earthly matters I walk over to a grey metal cubicle beneath a sign saying "*Toilette*" and study the instructions on the outside. An orange light informs me that it's occupied. Behind me a Japanese tourist leader is speaking to the flock gathered round her. With all the attractions around, why is she pointing at the toilet?

The curved door glides open, a woman comes out and the door closes again. Watery sounds from within signal the automatic washing, disinfecting and drying cycle of the interior, increasing the need for my interior to empty itself.

As soon as the green light comes on I insert my coin and press the button to open the door. I enter and turn to watch it close, somewhat bemused to see the Japanese tourists watching, nodding and smiling.

My anxiety increases as the voices outside grow louder and closer but it would take much more than this to stop my flow.

Quickly straightening my skirt, I pull on the handle to activate the door. I emerge, half dazzled by the daylight, to polite clapping from the tourists and grin awkwardly to conceal my embarrassment at having been an unwitting player in the leader's demonstration of how to use a French public toilet.

"Ah, there you are at last," Dennis reproaches, "We seem to spend a large chunk of our lives bogged down in the search for toilets."

Ignoring his comment, as I have for most of our married life, I join the queue for the funicular railway – a cable-hauled cabin that mounts the steep slope of *Montmartre*.

"I'm not going in that again. Too much like flying." A glance at his face tells me that Dennis is not joking. " I'm taking the steps. See you at the top."

The cabin exhales passengers to one side then inhales a fresh supply from the other. A red display above counts in thirty-five of us – the maximum allowed. Unlike on the buses and Métro, here there's a strictly enforced limit.

Dennis is waiting for me at the top, breathless and clutching his chest.

"See, it's faster to walk," he pants…

I feel a sudden thrill of anticipation as we enter the *Place du Tertre*. The sun is filtering through leafy trees onto artists at their easels. The smell of fresh oil paint and tobacco smoke hangs in the air. An artist calls to a skinny white puppy and throws it a piece of baguette.

The square isn't yet crowded with tourists. And with less pressure on the artists to perform, a couple are playing chess, while others are drinking coffee, chatting or arranging their displays.

An old man with a grey beard recognises me.

"Here she is, the Englishwoman who comes to spy on us," he remarks jovially and looks inquiringly at Dennis. "And you are her secretary?" Dennis, not understanding, nods and replies, "*Oui*."

I chuckle and translate for him. He shrugs.

"Well, you win some and you lose some. I reckon if I answer '*Oui*' to any question asked by a Frenchman, I've a fifty percent chance of being right. Unless, of course, it's the Police who are asking, in which case I'd deny everything."

My artist friend continues to smile affably.

We meander through the square, stopping often to observe artists' portraits. We discuss their likeness or otherwise to the adults posing self-consciously or children posing restlessly. Briefly, we're amateur art critics, alongside a steadily growing influx of tourists. Whatever must it be like to sit here day after day, with your artistic creations being constantly scrutinised by a stream of pseudo art connoisseurs, many of whom are oblivious or insensitive to the fact that your multilingual experiences mean you have a basic understanding of their comments? What a way to earn a living!

Leaving the artists behind we take the winding road down towards the nearest Métro station, *Abbesses*. A man approaching us looks vaguely familiar. As he gets closer I recognise Jean-Paul.

His face lights up.

"Ah, *bonjour, Madame*!"

He bends to kiss me on both cheeks.

"This is Jean-Paul, who mended our drill and advised me about insurance companies," I explain hurriedly to a somewhat surprised Dennis.

I introduce them to each other and they shake hands.

"I've been visiting friends nearby," Jean-Paul tells me. "What brings you up here?"

"We've been watching the artists," I enthuse.

"Like a true tourist." His tone is derisory. "The only Parisians you'll find there are those trying to make money out of you. If you like, we can meet next weekend and I'll show you both the *real* Paris, the one rarely seen by tourists. Sadly, though, I don't speak English. Please apologise to your husband for me."

Before I know it, we've arranged a meeting, a

time and a place for Saturday and exchanged phone numbers.

Dennis and I go into the attractive art deco entrance at *Abbesses* station and down the steep, seemingly endless spiral staircase, flanked on one side by colourful scenes of *Montmartre*. The arrival of a train gives us a chance to sit and relax, to listen to a busker with a gravelly voice, not unlike that of Edith Piaf, accompanying herself on an accordion. Dennis is studying his Métro map.

"Let's go to *Picpus*," he suggests. "I'd like to see what a place with such a ridiculous name looks like."

He works out a route.

Picpus turns out to be a quiet, respectable, principally residential area with well-established, elegant apartment blocks.

"I'm hungry, Dennis." I steer him towards a menu on a restaurant window. They don't do chicken and chips but we'll settle for omelettes.

Inside, we seat ourselves and an unsmiling waitress readies herself to write down our order.

"We'll have the omelettes," I tell her. "One with chips and the other with salad."

She gives us a withering look. "Sorry, Madame, it's lunchtime. We haven't got time to make you omelettes."

"What can we have then?" I ask, bewildered.

"*Croque Monsieur*," she replies offhandedly, turning on her heels to take (or perhaps reject) another customer's order.

"What did she say?" Dennis looks puzzled. "Why didn't she write down our order?"

"Apparently there isn't time to make omelettes. But she could get us a toasted sandwich with ham and cheese."

"Is this a restaurant or isn't it?" Dennis' loud sarcasm passes unheard or unheeded as we make a speedy exit in search of somewhere more convivial.

"You wouldn't believe this if you read it in a book, would you?" I remark.

There's another restaurant a few doors down. We dive in hungrily and select lamb chops from the menu.

"Cooked right through please, with no blood," I say firmly, knowing the French preference for rare-cooked meat and wanting Dennis to be impressed by Parisian cooking.

The waiter nods curtly, his face maintaining a stony impassivity.

"What's the matter? Why does nobody smile round here?" Dennis snaps at his departing back. "Is that what *Picpus* means? There I was, thinking it was a cartoon cat. Perhaps it should be renamed *Sourpuss*."

The waiter returns with cutlery, Dennis' beer and my wine.

Forty-five hungry minutes pass. The waiter slams two plates down in front of us. Is this his way of showing he enjoys his job?

"*Voila*!" His manner says, 'Take it or leave it. Makes no difference to me.'

"It's like they're doing us a favour by serving us," I say in exasperation.

We pick up our cutlery and cut into our chops. They're burnt on the outside but red raw inside. For my part, I quite like lamb rare. But this is neither one nor the other – it's just seared, uncooked meat.

I daren't look at Dennis' face. I know precisely what he's thinking and feeling.

"This isn't typical of French restaurants," I venture meekly.

But how on earth am I going to convince him after this?

Chapter *Dix-Huit*

I'm an artist in *Place du Tertre.*

The other artists are elbowing forward, each wanting to be the first to have their portrait done by me. To calm the situation I seat them in a semicircle, promising to do a picture of them all together. They're posing in black and white, beaming happily at me. They make a splendid group, sitting dead still, waiting patiently for me to begin.

I select a pastel. My hand is poised to make the first stroke on the paper…

One of the artists is leaning forward, pulling hard on my foot.

"Get off!" I shout angrily.

"Sorry!" The voice sounds vaguely familiar.

The artists are dissolving into a white mist.

Dennis is kneeling on my foot in his effort to clamber over me and down the mezzanine ladder.

I don't have many such vividly beautiful dreams. Trust him to interrupt it!

We rush through breakfast to be in time for our appointment with Jean-Paul.

"It's an organised walk, starting at ten. Please don't be late," he said when he rang to confirm it yesterday evening.

No lie in for us today!

Hurrying towards the Métro, I hear strains of the 1812 Overture – the new ringtone Nikki set up for me. I take my mobile phone from my pocket.

"Mum – guess what? I had my first driving lesson at five thirty this morning. My instructor said it would be the quietest time."

"And was it?" I can't think what else to say to this news. Why would anyone want to drive in Paris?

"Yes. I've never seen Paris that deserted."

"How did it go?"

"Scary. It's an intensive course. We were out for two hours. We covered a lot of the city."

"Rather you than me," I say, shrinking from the very idea. What if the intensive course leads to Intensive Care?

On the train, I relay the gist of our conversation to Dennis.

"It doesn't bear thinking about," he says. "My daughter, about to join the ranks of French homicidal drivers…"

Jean-Paul, true to his word, is waiting at the *Hôtel de Ville* – Paris' City Hall. He stoops to embrace me on both cheeks and shake Dennis' hand. Either he's particularly tall or we're shrinking.

"We are meeting round the corner. Follow me." He sets off at a brisk pace, with Dennis and me half running down the street behind him. We round a corner. Jean-Paul doesn't stop. We trot after him down a long street and turn several more corners. He slows to a halt opposite a group of about a dozen people.

"Here we are," he tells us.

We cross the road and join them. A scholarly-faced man carrying a clipboard nods to Jean-Paul, who introduces him as our guide.

We're a motley collection, with Jean-Paul

towering above everyone else: two hippie-looking women, engrossed in their guidebooks, an elderly woman looking like she's come straight from a supermarket with her bulging bags, a handful who look like students; and us – fish (or is that *poissons*?) out of water.

*

We've now been on this tour for an hour and a half, if you can call long stretches of standing about a 'tour.' I've given up any pretence of looking interested in the guide's droning commentary about the historical significance of the local architecture. Initially, I actually enjoyed viewing plush apartment blocks above eye-level and studying intricate ironwork adorning balconies and window ledges. And when our guide drew our attention to the small, unadorned rooftop rooms – servants' quarters in earlier days, momentarily I was back forty years. The Spanish maid who worked for the family where I was a nanny had just such basic accommodation but worse, owing to her lowly status, was barred from using the lift, obliged to access her room by plodding up six flights of stairs…

Now my neck is painful from looking constantly upwards, my feet are solid blocks of wood and my bladder is overly full.

Dennis, understanding nothing of the lengthy explanations, is amusing himself, and embarrassing me, with his sarcastic remarks about everything in sight; he's either ignorant of or past caring about any impression he's giving to our companions.

While Jean-Paul is peering eagerly over his spectacles, giving his own superfluous nuggets of information to no one in particular.

"I have to use a toilet," I whisper to him loudly in French. My urgent tone breaks the spell. He grabs my arm and hurries me along the street, followed by a bewildered Dennis.

"In here," Jean-Paul says, pointing to a bar.

"But I don't want a drink," I protest.

"Quickly, go to the toilet," he orders. "I'll have an espresso."

I can't recall when I was last so relieved to see the welcoming word, '*Toilettes.*' I push open the swing door. A man in full flow casts me a scornful look over his shoulder.

"*Pardon.*" I back out and locate the door marked, '*Femmes'*.

Congratulating myself on successfully using the hole-in-the-floor toilet without wetting myself or my clothes, I take hold of the doorknob. It comes off in my hand. It won't fix back on. I stare at it blankly.

I'm trapped, banged up in this smelly little cubicle. I hammer wildly on the door and listen in vain for a response. Surely someone else must use a toilet here?

"How much longer are you going to be?"

What a convenient moment for Dennis to manifest his impatient nature!

"I'm stuck. The doorknob's come off. Can you get someone to break in?"

"How am I going to tell them all that? Do you expect me to mime your dilemma?"

"Dennis, listen. I'll tell you what to say in French. You can repeat it and memorize it."

"I'll have a go." He sounds half-hearted.

"*La poignet de la porte des toilettes s' est cassée.*" I enunciate each word
slowly. "That means 'the toilet doorknob is broken.'"

Grimacing at his strongly anglicised rendering as he plays it back to me, I continue.

"*Ma femme n'arrive pas a sortir.* 'My wife can't get out.'"

He practices these sentences several times.

"That'll do," I say, attempting to galvanize him into action and hoping he'll make himself understood.

Minutes later, I hear footsteps.

"Polly, it's Jean-Paul. What's the problem? Dennis is trying to tell me something and waving his hands in this direction. Are you ill?"

"No, I'm locked in. The doorknob's come off."

"I'll soon have you out," he assures me confidently.

I can hear him fiddling with something on the door, but to no avail. Finally admitting defeat he goes off for reinforcements, shouting, "Wait a minute, Polly!"

What else does he think I can do – slide under the two-inch gap beneath the door?

My frayed nerves have refilled my bladder.

I fasten my jeans quickly as the noise of scraping metal and another male voice herald the possibility of imminent rescue.

The door opens. A contrite waiter issues a

stream of apologies as I make an ungainly exit.

Jean-Paul and Dennis are laughing uproariously in the bar. I assume I'm the butt of their joke.

"I'm glad you find it so amusing," I reproach Dennis.

"Well, I always imagined that being locked in a loo was your idea of paradise!" He roars with laughter. "I haven't laughed so much for ages. The tears are rolling down my legs!"

I storm outside. Both men follow, wiping their eyes.

"You deserve a treat after that," Jean-Paul says kindly. "I'm taking you somewhere special for lunch. I have tickets for a typically French meal in the restaurant of a top school for hoteliers."

Dennis' eyes widen in horror when I translate.

But Jean-Paul is already striding towards the Métro.

Coming out of another station into the *Avenue de Clichy*, we accompany Jean-Paul to a rather anonymous-looking building. Upstairs we find ourselves in a small foyer where we are greeted immediately and ushered into the large, formal but comfortable dining area. My chair is pulled back for me to be seated. A neat, colourful posy of flowers graces the centre of a beautifully laid table and a uniformed waiter presents us with the Menu of the Day.

Jean-Paul is perusing his menu thoughtfully.

Dennis keeps glancing meaningfully at me and nudging my knee with his.

"Is there anything remotely edible?" he hisses in my ear.

"You have to accept what they give you for the entrée and dessert but there's a choice for the main dish. Remember, this is a school – there's not a wide choice. You could have lamb medallions with garlic. But since you can't stand garlic or rare meat you're probably better off with the eggs and mushrooms *au gratin* – that's topped with melted, grated cheese."

The waiter returns.

"Madame and I will have the lamb," Jean-Paul informs him.

"Dennis wants the vegetarian option," I add quickly, offended that Jean-Paul has already seen fit to choose on my behalf.

The wine waiter arrives with the half-bottle of red wine Jean-Paul has ordered and pours a little into his glass. He sniffs pensively before sipping it.

"This is a very fine wine," he tells us, as proudly as if he'd produced it himself.

Dennis' suntanned face turns a strange colour as the starter is placed in front of him – salmon mousse with capers. Jean-Paul and I tuck in hungrily.

"Delicious!" I announce, hoping Jean-Paul won't notice Dennis pushing capers to the edge of his plate and toying with his mousse.

His lack of enthusiasm for the main course does not, however, pass unnoticed.

"Dennis has not touched his food or wine. Is he all right?" Jean-Paul looks concerned.

I pass the question on, suppressing my urge to laugh at the sickly grin on Dennis' face. He deserves this for making fun of my toilet troubles earlier.

"Tell him I think I have a stomach virus – maybe it was the chicken and chips I ate yesterday."

"Ah, the English – they always eat what is bad for them," Jean-Paul says knowingly.

Thank goodness Dennis is keeping his views on French cuisine to himself – though no doubt I'll hear them later! And I already know that when it comes to wine he claims to have tone-deaf tastebuds.

He does, however, manage to eat every single one of his chocolate profiteroles and drink his espresso!

I thank Jean-Paul profusely for the meal that I, at least, enjoyed.

"Do you like flowers, Polly?"

"Er – yes," I falter, wondering how Dennis will react to a strange Frenchman presenting me with a bouquet.

"Good. I'm taking you now to a wonderful garden with beautiful plants from around the world. Then this evening we are going to a concert in an extraordinary setting. You both like classical music, don't you?"

A rhetorical question, as he continues, as though thinking out loud, "There are two possible routes to our destination. We can go by bus or Métro."

"I prefer bus rides – you get to see more," I suggest with enthusiasm.

"The Métro is better. It's quicker," he concludes, heading in that direction, appearing not to have heard me and clearly expecting us to follow him.

"What's happening?" Dennis hasn't a clue what Jean-Paul said.

"He's organised some really interesting events for us. Isn't that kind? I think you'll enjoy the evening especially."

"Presumably we have no choice?"

"Shhhh! He might hear you. It could spoil the *Entente Cordiale.*"

"What's that, some kind of drink?"

We run to catch up with Jean-Paul.

At *Boulogne Pont de St Cloud* we exit the Métro. We're in a leafy area on the west side of Paris, its great expanse of visible blue sky giving it a decidedly countrified feel. Jean-Paul strides purposefully ahead with us almost running to keep up. Entering an attractive, compact building he purchases tickets. The discreetly lit room is surrounded by an open gallery. On both levels an exhibition of early twentieth century photographs depicting scenes of North Africa looks strangely at odds with its ultra-modern environment.

Remarkably, Jean-Paul and Dennis are managing to communicate their shared passion for photography through a series of rapidly changing facial expressions, exaggerated hand movements and the occasional word or phrase.

"Wait until you see the garden," Jean-Paul says, leading us into the open air.

Tastefully landscaped, with a variety of strategically planted shrubs and trees, narrow bridges spanning trickling streams and ablaze with every imaginable kind of flowering plant, this garden is a *tour de force*. Jean-Paul says its designer, Albert Kahn, after whom the garden is named, was a philanthropist who wanted to create a harmonious blend of the best of Japanese, British, French and other styles. He also collected the photographs in the exhibition, realising that they showed a world soon to disappear.

I could wander in blissful silence for hours through this wonderland with its meandering maze of sun-dappled, pebbled pathways, its hidden walkways reminiscent of mountain tracks and its pagodas and Japanese teahouses.

But Jean-Paul is keen to impart some of his extensive horticultural knowledge. I have little option but to listen to (or, more truthfully, be bored rigid by) his lengthy lectures about the history and cultivation of individual plants.

I'm reminded of the chorus of a song I heard as a child.

'*Inch worm, inch worm*
Measuring the marigolds
Seems to me you'd stop and see
How beautiful they are…'

A downward glance at my watch shows I've been rooted to this spot for twenty minutes. I excuse myself to look for a toilet, feeling envious of Dennis, whose lack of French enables him to wander off with impunity.

I amble back, breathing in the warmth of the day hanging sweet in the air, content to revel in the sensation of the sun on my skin and the pure beauty around me.

"There you are!" Jean-Paul's voice startles me.

"Come and look at the fruit trees in the orchard."

Dennis has reappeared to see what we're doing next. I take his hand and hold onto it tightly. If I must endure Jean-Paul's ramblings, so will he!

The orchard is not what I expected. Instead of a field with randomly placed fruit trees, this is an organised system of plants, which have been trained in bizarre shapes, horizontally along wire fencing and up metal poles.

I reach out and touch a perfect, fully ripened apple…

"Don't do that! Its not allowed!" I freeze at Jean-Paul's sudden, fierce outburst. I withdraw my trembling hand feeling as guilty as Eve in the Garden of Eden. Passers-by looked shocked and disapproving, either by Jean-Paul shouting, my touching forbidden fruit, or both.

Jean-Paul turns on his heels, ducks under an archway with us in tow and takes a short cut across the lawn to an exit, oblivious to or ignoring the sign prohibiting walking on the grass.

*

Regular meals are not on our new French friend's agenda. Lunch was six hours ago. We've walked for miles and my stomach is rumbling as we stand in a queue for tickets for tonight's concert.

"I'm hungry and thirsty," I complain.

"Ok, we'll look for a café, Jean-Paul assures me.

We're in the *Serres d'Auteuil*, another of Paris'

delightful gardens, with large greenhouses full of rare plants from around the world, impeccable beds of well-tended roses and green carpets of untrodden lawns (Keep Off The Grass is an inflexible rule here).

Abandoning our futile search for refreshments, we go into the grandest of greenhouses with a piano on a dais at one end and giant tropical plants surrounding rows of seats filled almost to capacity. The air is hot and humid. It's a relief to sit down.

An American pianist enters to applause, sits at the piano and begins to play…

We've enjoyed the concert in what turned out to be a surprisingly good acoustic. Jean-Paul certainly got this bit of the day right. He tells us that this and other gardens around Paris are regular venues for concerts with musical treats for all tastes.

Outside, Dennis points out the Roland Garros Tennis Club across the road, describing it as France's counterpart to Wimbledon. Turning a corner, I see we're leaving the *Avenue Gordon Bennett.* I draw Dennis' attention to the street sign.

"Gordon Bennett!" he exclaims.

Jean-Paul can't understand why we're laughing and I'm not sure how to explain why it's funny. So I don't.

On the train back into the city I find out more about Jean-Paul's life. He comes from a well-off family whom he rarely sees, lives alone and has a small circle of friends.

"When are you returning to Paris?" he asks.

"Probably not before January. There's a lot happening between now and then."

"Do you have your whole family at home for Christmas?"

"Yes, we usually do. What are you doing?"

"I have no idea. I may visit a friend."

"Well, if all else fails you can pop over to England," I say casually.

He asks me for my English phone number and I see no harm in giving him it. It's unlikely he'll use it.

He gets off the train at the next station and we turn our minds to something important – where are we going to eat?

Chapter *Dix-Neuf*

The glittering Christmas lights still adorning Parisian streets do little to dispel the gloom that January's heavy clouds throw over everything and everyone. The air carries the threat of rain; but worse is the thought of a phone call from Jean-Paul.

'All else' *did* fail as, shortly before Christmas, Jean-Paul rang asking for our address saying he wanted to take us up on our kind offer.

How could I tell him it was only a throwaway remark?

But if nothing else, his weeklong stay was an interesting interlude in our lives and we glimpsed ourselves and our culture from a French perspective. Jean-Paul generously expressed his appreciation with a present of quality wines bottled in prestigious French vineyards and showed an enthusiastic interest in our local historical architecture. And our son's valiant attempts to teach him English were amply rewarded when Jean-Paul adopted "Hello Mate" as a regular greeting.

But his pompous denunciations of English food were more than a match for Dennis' opinions of French cuisine. His "*Ah, merde!*" on sampling Bisto and Marmite made him an unlikely first choice to spearhead their makers' future publicity campaigns. And his persistent efforts to reconstruct my Christmas Day menu by repeated interference, in the hope of raising my culinary expertise from its English depths to the exalted level of the French, resulted in banishment from my kitchen. Thereafter, he retreated to the lounge where he and

Dennis steeped themselves in excruciatingly loud jazz.

I'm diverted back to the present by the enticing smell of hot roasting chestnuts. The seller is turning them constantly on a perforated metal tray balanced on a giant canister of glowing coals in a supermarket trolley. These chestnut roasters are on practically every street corner of the city in wintertime. Are there any trolleys left in the supermarkets? Do they beg, borrow or steal them?

I buy a bag of piping hot chestnuts, willing him not to select the burnt ones.

My mobile rings.

"Polly, where are you? How are you getting on with your insurance? Do you need my help?"

"It's Jean-Paul," I whisper to Dennis, whose eyes roll back in his head.

"Tell him we're not here."

"Don't be silly!" I hiss back, covering the mouthpiece.

"Yes, please, Jean-Paul, I'd welcome your help with the insurance. It might speed things up. In fact we're on our way there now. We're outside our local Commercial Centre."

"Good. I'll meet you at the entrance in ten minutes or so."

Jean-Paul doesn't keep us waiting. He hastens towards us, kisses us both and greets Dennis with "Hello, Mate!"

"Here's a little surprise for you both," he announces, handing me a box. "It's a French speciality. We call it *La Galette des Rois.* It's made of puff pastry and celebrates the Three Kings who followed the star to find the Baby Jesus. Carry it carefully, Polly. You don't want to crush it. Now let's go and I'll deal with your insurance before I attend my dental appointment."

My gratitude is tempered by annoyance at being spoken to like a small child. I have to remind myself that it's just Jean-Paul's way, though it doesn't make it easier to take. I do, however, bow to his superior knowledge of the world of French insurance, which differs from the English like many things French.

The usual cordial chorus of "*bonjour,*" heralds our entry into the insurance office, where my agent proffers her hand.

"How is the weather in England?" she asks. I now realise that this is a subtle French joke: they think the English preoccupation with the weather is funny.

As I open my mouth to reply with what I hope is a witty response, Jean-Paul interrupts.

"When is this Expert coming to visit Madame?" he demands.

The agent's friendly smile disappears. She's quite evidently taken aback as he launches into a ferocious tirade against the speed of insurance settlements in general and this one in particular.

Instantly I regret bringing him here. I naively imagined that a French person who understood French bureaucracy would be better at handling this than an English person who didn't. But I reckoned without Jean-Paul.

I want to intervene, to apologise for bringing this strange man into the office but his speech is seamless in its flow.

The agent's face has drained of blood. She's mesmerised, shocked by his endless stream of words and patronising tone. The rest of the staff are staring at him, frozen behind their desks.

Jean-Paul looks calm and serious and hasn't once raised his voice above normal speaking level. Dennis looks perfectly unflustered. As far as he's concerned Jean-Paul is helping us resolve a complicated problem.

His message rammed home, Jean-Paul takes a deep breath and looks pointedly down at the agent.

"Come with me Madame." She takes me gently but firmly by the arm to her desk. "The Expert went to your apartment in November. He didn't get the message that you were not in France and asked me to contact him when I knew you were returning. Here is the fax I received this morning from the Expert in response to you contacting me last week before you left England. He has arranged to visit your apartment on Friday morning at ten o'clock. Does that time suit you?" she asks with frosty politeness.

"Yes, absolutely. Thank you so much," I say, shaking her hand. The rest of my body is shaking with fury at Jean-Paul's obnoxious behaviour.

We walk out, past the still statuesque, silent figures behind desks.

"You see? That's how it's done. I spurred her into action," Jean-Paul states smugly. "We French know how to handle bureaucrats."

He must have misinterpreted the agent's reaction. Can't he feel my anger? Dennis can.

He's looking perplexed. I can't bring myself to thank Jean-Paul for making a difficult situation worse.

"I'm late for my dentist." Jean-Paul embraces us hastily and disappears down the steps to the Métro.

It's hardly surprising he has a small circle of friends. And it's probably just shrunk by one – or two, if you count Dennis.

I explain the scene in the office to enlighten Dennis.

"I think we'd best pop in tomorrow and apologise," he says. "We can't afford to alienate them at this stage."

"Really? Then when *should* we alienate them?"

Dennis knows when it's best to let a subject drop.

We turn our minds to pleasanter thoughts. We're going to the most renowned of Paris' *Marchés aux Puces*, or Flea Markets, at *St Ouen*.

Coming out of the Métro at *Porte de Clignancourt*, an area with a slightly seedy feel, we cross a road that runs under the *Périphérique*, the Paris equivalent of the M25.

Approaching the market, Dennis regurgitates a morsel of the guidebook he's been digesting since breakfast.

"In the middle ages, peasants sold garments discarded by the rich and riddled with fleas. That's how the markets became known as *Puces* – Flea Markets."

I allow myself a secret smile of satisfaction.

Dennis, who generally extols the virtues of everything English, has been reading and showing a marked enthusiasm for facts and figures about this seductive city. He's been won over! He's even discovered a cure for his occasional insomnia – he learns Métro lines from one end to the other, reciting each station in order with careful attention to pronunciation.

This is not the usual kind of market. Admittedly, there are stalls selling clothes, leather goods, hardware and other items you'd expect to find in any market. But this one is exceptional because of its small shops selling antiques or bric-a-brac, areas resembling shopping arcades and entire streets with one kind of product, like antiques, electrical paraphernalia or wartime memorabilia.

I've heard you can buy anything here. And given the length and breadth of this complex, I can well believe it. I'm sure it's possible to wander its alleyways, streets and covered spaces for hours, without once retracing my steps.

I pick up a hand-carved, polished wooden tortoise.

"I'm buying this for Fran," I tell Dennis. "If I don't get it now I'll never find my way back here."

Many traders are friendly and chatty and I'm happy to indulge my love of French.

"What time do you start each day?" I ask one.

"I'm here at seven in the morning until seven at night, whatever the weather."

I shiver at the thought of standing here in rain, wind and snow to eke out a living. But our time in the *Puces* has lifted my spirits and the incident with

Jean-Paul has faded into insignificance.

As we're going back to the Métro my phone vibrates. I answer it reluctantly. It might be *him* again, organising the rest of our day if not the rest of our lives.

"Hi, is that Polly?" A female voice I don't recognise addresses me in English.

"Yes, who's that?" I ask bluntly.

"It's Ruby. Remember me? We met on the Eurostar train to London last September."

Instantly I recall the outgoing, retired American couple we got chatting to. They too have a Paris apartment and we exchanged French mobile numbers, intending to meet up sometime.

"Ruby! Of course! How are you?"

"We're fine. We're round your part of Paris early this evening. How about we drop by for a coffee?" she drawls.

We've arranged for Olivier, our neighbour, to come round at eight, so I suggest they visit about five. I give her our address and the entrance code.

"So the Americans are invading tonight," says Dennis.

"Try to keep off politics," I warn, knowing how contentious he can be.

We grab a quick baguette from a bakery before returning to the apartment. I tap in the code to the building, knowing I have half an hour to get everything ready for our visitors. But they've beaten us to it. They're beaming at us from our landing.

"Hi! I know we're early, but hey! It's good to see you again."

"You too," I say, ushering them into our apartment, into the salon and onto the sofa.

You have such a cute little place here!" Ruby enthuses.

What's *his* name? I search my empty brain frantically.

"Don't they, Archie?" she continues, resolving my dilemma.

"Right, will you have tea or coffee?" I ask.

Ruby hesitates before answering. "Archie will have coffee but I'll have wine," she decides, indicating the bottle of vintage wine – a birthday present from Nikki – on the table.

She can't be serious! It's afternoon teatime! But knowing how hospitable Americans are when at home and not wishing to give offence, I hand Dennis a corkscrew and ask him to do the honours whilst I see to the rest of the refreshments. I carefully remove the *galette* from its box. On top lies a shiny gold cardboard crown. It's obviously part of a custom I know little (in fact, nothing) about. I slice the *galette* with difficulty (and a knife) and warm it in the microwave to serve with our drinks.

Dennis gets into an intense political discussion with Archie, while Ruby talks *at* me about life, the universe and everything in between.

Munching my slice of *galette*, I relish the light flakiness of the pastry, and delicious marzipan flavouring inside. But all of a sudden I bite down on something hard in my mouth. My first thought is that a tooth has broken or a filling come loose.

Hearing my sudden cry, Dennis looks across at

me.

"What's the matter?"

I spit the hard object into my hand. It's a tiny china figurine.

"How did that get there?" I gulp, holding up the offending item for all to see.

"It's either part of a ritual or a French attempt to finish off the English," Dennis suggests unhelpfully.

I'm relieved to find that all my teeth, as well as the ornament, are still intact and make a mental note to ask Olivier about *galettes*.

In the meantime, Ruby, oblivious to what's happening around her, has helped herself to another large glass of wine. She pours yet another… and the bottle is drained.

That was my present that was…

Dennis and Archie have moved on to an intellectual discourse about American music. Ruby, meanwhile, has dried up verbally.

I offer the men more tea.

"Please don't give my wife any more wine. She's had enough." Archie intercepts as Ruby opens her mouth to speak. "In fact, it's time we were going," he adds hurriedly.

Ruby stands unsteadily and they leave, promising (or threatening?) to return. As they descend the stairs I'm grateful that I have American friends and relatives, knowing that it would be too easy to stereotype an entire nationality on the basis of a short acquaintance.

Coffee with Olivier is an altogether different experience. He's asks how we're settling in and bravely seeks out our English feelings about Paris in general and Parisians in particular. I mention my struggle to understand the workings of insurance in France.

"Bureaucracy here is hard enough for the French. We have far too much paperwork and information about anything can vary, depending on which official you consult. I cannot begin to imagine how you cope," he empathises.

He's amused by my account of the *galette* incident.

"Your friend should have informed you about the *fève* hidden inside when it's baked. Whoever finds it gets to wear the crown."

"I bet French dentists make a great living out of this tradition," Dennis ventures, when I explain.

Olivier shares his excitement about his forthcoming marriage and as we show him out he invites us to an evening at his place to meet his fiancée.

"Don't hesitate to call on me if I can be of any assistance," he offers, opening his door.

Olivier has completely restored my faith in human nature, especially that of the French variety.

*

"If the Insurance agent was right, Dennis, we should get a visit this morning from –"

The doorbell rings.

"*C'est qui?*" I shout from the kitchen.

"*L'Expert, Madame.*"

I glance at the clock. Friday, 10 a.m. on the dot,

as promised. A good timekeeper, this Expert.

I open the door to a smartly dressed, clean-shaven young man.

"*Bonjour, Madame.*" He smiles politely and enters with clipboard and pen.

I take him on a tour of inspection. Businesslike, he silently measures the uneven, misshapen floorboards, tests the humidity levels in discoloured, flaking walls and makes copious notes.

Preferring not to dwell on these sad aspects of our little investment I console myself with thoughts of its eventual transformation. By the time the Expert departs I've conjured up a residence fit for royalty. Mind you, remembering what the French did to their last royals, maybe I'd better tone the image down somewhat!

Chapter *Vingt*

We venture out into a steady, unpleasant drizzle, the kind of weather that leaves you very damp, slightly steaming and rather dejected.

Figuring that the price of a meal in the *Louvre* – our focus for the day, since it's the first Sunday of the month – would nearly bankrupt us, I've made a packed lunch.

We squash into a Métro train bursting at the seams, where I crane my neck, looking for spare seats but can't see any. Where has everyone come from?

It's taken half an hour to reach the station grandly named *Palais Royal – Musée du Louvre*, where we spill out onto the platform alongside most of the train's passengers. Either Parisians are a truly cultured lot or this is a convenient excuse to get out of the cramped apartments in which many of them live.

We follow the flow of bodies past expensive shops in the arcade that leads into the *Louvre*. Although the queue is immense and the entrance out of sight there is a continuous, if slow, forward movement.

"Oh, NO!" Dennis exclaims.

"What?" I'm concerned to see him clutching his head. A trip to hospital is not my idea of a day out.

"You know that carrier bag you put the sandwiches in? "

"You've forgotten it." It wouldn't be the first time Dennis has forgotten something. Birthdays, anniversaries, appointments…

He looks guilty. "Worse. I picked it up with the rubbish bag I was taking down to the backyard. I must have thrown them both in the bin together."

"There go my lovingly prepared cheese and pickle sandwiches," I remark mournfully.

He looks genuinely remorseful. "I'm sorry, love."

"Just don't complain about French food today."

Reaching the front Dennis is asked to remove his backpack for scanning. This formality over, we pick up maps to help us find our way through this incredibly complex building.

"I must find a loo," I tell him impatiently.

"Hang on, I'll check the map," he replies.

But I've already spotted a queue of women standing below the international symbols that show me where I need to be.

Twenty-five minutes waiting here has intensified my need for a toilet. And I'm not the only one in this state. The whole queue is jigging up and down on the spot in a weird, primitive, minimalistic dance. We women are obliged to watch the men breezing in and out at speed while we exercise extreme muscular control. How unfair! I'm strongly tempted to break ranks and use the men's toilet. I've done it before.

Dennis, unusually for him, is not pacing around looking at his watch and hasn't noticed my return. Instead, his eyes are fixed on the expanse of glass and steel that form a pyramid over this vast concourse, startling in its modernity against the backdrop of these ancient, historic buildings.

Beneath it hundreds, maybe thousands, of visitors mill about in chaotic orderliness.

I give up trying to fathom out the complicated outlay on my map to follow Dennis, whose sense of direction is infinitely superior to mine.

We arrive in a huge room lined from floor to ceiling with elaborately framed paintings. The mass of people who poured into the *Louvre* with us has melted away.

"I bet they've gone to photograph the Mona Lisa," Dennis decides.

I'm intrigued by a fifteenth century painting of the Martyrdom of Saint Sebastian in which he looks as if he's posing casually, totally unmoved by the whole experience despite the arrows piercing his body. Where's the anguish?

"Look at his face," I say to Dennis in disbelief. "How can he look so nonchalant? He looks like he's bored to death."

"So would you if you'd been here all these years. Anyway, he probably knows he's on display and doesn't want to depress people." Dennis' has this remarkable ability to trivialise anything, even the greatest of masterpieces.

Abandoning the map, which has managed to defeat us both, we find ourselves on a gallery overlooking a large, airy, glass-covered quadrangle with huge, impressive sculptures and white stone benches.

"That's where Fran and I ate our sandwiches," I tell him, pointing to a corner bench.

"What an amazingly intellectual pair you are," he comments dryly.

We continue through an interminable series of halls, rooms and galleries filled with an astounding assortment of famous masterpieces by great artists throughout the centuries. They range from exquisite miniatures you could fit in a handbag to expansive canvases reaching the entire height of the walls and tapestries stretching the whole length of rooms. Many of the paintings are so familiar; and these are the originals, touched by the artists' living hands – Rembrandt, Botticelli, Monet…

For a while we're spellbound, lost in time and admiration.

My feet drag me back to the present, refusing to carry me further. I plonk my tired, aching body onto one of the padded seats in the middle of the room, content to view the art from a distance. Dennis, meanwhile, is closely examining Arcimboldo's colourful, surrealistic depictions of the seasons, with faces composed of fruit, leaves and vegetables.

The gurgling in my stomach urges me to bring Dennis down to more mundane matters.

"Shall we get something to eat?" I suggest.

We begin a lengthy search for a restaurant, asking directions from people who are as confused as we are, before finding a security guard who directs us to a café where muffins and coffee are the most we can afford.

Sufficiently rested and partially refuelled, we explore the palatial suite of Emperor Napoleon III, for whom money was clearly not a concern. But the sight of a lavishly laid table complete with everything except food leaves me hungry, irritable and ready for home.

"We must see the Mona Lisa before we go," Dennis says hurriedly, noticing my marked change of mood. *His* legs seem to have found a new lease of life.

Via a series of false turns, infuriatingly inaccurate directions and lucky guesses in this irregular, complicated maze, we enter yet another enormous, high-ceilinged room where initially, the world's most well-known painting is evident only by crowds of tourists flashing cameras in its general direction.

"Where is it?" Dennis asks me.

"It's the other side of all these people on a wall of its own," I tell him in a hushed voice. "Where those security guards are."

As bodies gradually disperse, we edge closer to the picture.

"So that's it, is it?" Dennis sounds distinctly disappointed and positively dismissive. "Bit small, isn't it? Can't understand all the fuss. Vermeer's Girl With a Pearl Earring is far more beautiful but doesn't attract half as much attention."

"It's the eyes," I suggest. "They seem to follow you wherever you go."

"So what? How does that make it great? I'm not impressed by the emperor's new clothes."

When Dennis has a bee in his bonnet about something, his voice increases considerably in pitch and volume. And his loud, irreverent opinionising is attracting outraged glares from international admirers of da Vinci's work.

Highly embarrassed, I steer him with some

difficulty towards the exit and out to the Métro.

A train tightly packed with standing passengers reluctant to shift still closer together is no easy challenge for any weary, would-be traveller to enter. But as the doors slide shut behind my back I'm determined as ever to reach the empty seat I can see everyone ignoring.

"*Pardon,*" I mumble, sliding sideways, tripping on an outstretched leg and pretending not to notice the annoyed faces. I'm past being bothered by what anyone thinks. I need to sit down.

The woman beside me is engrossed in a novel. Fairly recently, too lazy to carry my own reading material, I've acquired the habit of reading snippets from magazines, books and newspapers over fellow-travellers' shoulders – everything from the Bible and the Koran to advertisements and weather reports. I once saw instructions for making French onion soup but unfortunately missed the crucial part of the recipe as I'd only got as far as "Cut the onions…" when the man beside me became aware of my nosiness, stared at me irately, folded his newspaper and tucked it under his arm. This and similar experiences shamed me into developing a more discreet method of this visual equivalent of eavesdropping. I hold my head facing forwards and, through half-closed eyelids, swivel my eyes until the page comes into view.

Using my newly developed skill, I begin reading, no longer having to translate as I go…

'That evening, Dominique was returning to Toulouse when he lost control of his car. He was burnt alive beside his wife when it turned over

several times…'

The books snaps shut without warning. Suddenly realising this is her stop the woman puts it in her bag, jumps up and hurries off the train, leaving me crestfallen, cheated and unfulfilled. I don't even know the book's title. The only way I'll know how it ends is if I write it myself.

Chapter *Vingt-et-Un*

Where better to be in springtime than here in Paris? And sipping my coffee on a café terrace I have a further reason to feel elated.

I've just heard one of the best bits of news in years: there's now free entry to every Parisian public toilet! I can't believe my luck. Ducking behind trees, bushes and under bridges is a thing of the past.

I can pee free whenever I want! I want to shout it to the world, accompanied by a fanfare of trumpets.

Hand in hand, Dennis and I are exploring a particularly vibrant part of Paris, where prestigious shops, chic boutiques and classy hotels abound in a confusion of streets around St Lazare station. This is Paris' answer to London's West End.

I don't know how long we've been walking but I do know this: I need a toilet – and soon!

Momentarily, I'm distracted by an extraordinary sight. Fronted by giant stone columns is what appears to be a Greek temple.

"What's this place?" I muse, more to myself than to Dennis.

"From the name of the Métro station over there, I'd say it was the Church of the Madeleine." Dennis points across the road.

But between us and the station is what I most wanted to see – a flight of stairs leading below street level to – Toilettes.

It doesn't feel anything like a public toilet, certainly not your bog-standard lavatory. Even at street level it's something special, with colourful mosaics lining the walls. And from the bottom step I look into a deserted, beautifully decorated lobby with healthy green plants and a white-tiled floor you could eat off. I push open one of the shiny wooden doors, feeling like Goldilocks intruding on the Three Bears' toilet ("Who's been sitting on MY loo?").

The interior is stunning. On the wall beside a spotless toilet above a delicate, shell-shaped sink, is a wooden-framed, oval mirror. And there are polished brass hooks on the back of the door, for hanging coats and handbags.

Only the modern, wall-mounted hand-dryer jars with the old-worldly charm of this little room filled with light flooding in through the coloured stained-glass window above the closed door.

It's like being in an en-suite of a five-star hotel, minus only the shower.

Coming out I half expect to see a reception desk with personnel in smart uniforms. But there's still just me.

Suddenly, I remember that Dennis is waiting.

"Did you enjoy your holiday?" he sniggers. "If I hadn't known there's only one entrance and exit I'd have thought you'd been kidnapped for the slave trade."

"I discovered Toilet Paradise," I gush. "If I'd had a book, sandwiches and a bottle of water, I'd have spent the day there." Sometimes I play Dennis at his own game.

The steps of the Métro are conveniently sited next to the toilets.

At the station barrier I take out my newly acquired Navigo pass, the plastic card that's replaced the Carte Orange, and place it against the scanner to open the barrier. Something's wrong.

The barrier remains closed. It can't have registered. I try again. And again.

There's never an official around when you want one. For a long frustrating minute I stare helplessly at Dennis on the other side. He got through so the machine must be working.

"Squeeze in with another passenger," he suggests.

When a thin young woman gains entry I flatten myself against her back. The turnstile revolves, letting us through as one. I've often seen others use this scam to get a free ride but I've never tried it myself.

The woman turns and glares at my audacity. Perhaps I should have asked her first. Too late to explain now. I grin back sheepishly.

At Duroc, another station we've picked at random, we refuel with coffees and pastries. On the wall behind Dennis is a poster advertising a free art exhibition with Venice as its main theme.

Although we have an appointment later on this afternoon we decide that this is unmissable. I ask another customer for directions and as luck would have it, it's in the next street.

Instead of the large public building we'd anticipated it's a small, privately owned gallery. A formally dressed woman greets us, introducing herself as the Director. Her self-important air leaves us in no doubt that this title needs a capital letter. She ushers us in, takes our coats and hands them to a cloakroom attendant.

"Would you like a glass of champagne before I show you round?" she offers, handing us glasses without waiting for a reply.

"This is certainly remarkably hospitable," Dennis comments.

"Hmm," is all I can muster. I'm beginning to realise something he obviously hasn't…

She escorts us into a room with a deep pile carpet, dark leather settee and antique writing bureau. The window looks out onto a flower-filled garden with freshly mown lawns.

A golden-framed pastel of Venice's Grand Canal at sunset – so convincing it looks like a photograph – graces one wall. I study the detail on the water closely.

"Amazing! The artist must surely be world famous," I suggest.

"Not yet. But he will be," the Director informs me. "You are fortunate to be able to buy it at today's reasonable price of four thousand, five hundred Euros, the promotional price for the exhibition, which finishes today."

"That's incredible!" I swallow hard, trying to conceal my shock at the price. At a quarter of that I couldn't afford it.

"Dennis, it's a mere four and a half thousand Euros."

"Oh. Really?" He looks lost for words. Is he beginning to catch on?

The Director is rubbing her hands, nodding encouragingly and smiling at us. Perhaps she's decided that a sale is imminent. She resumes the tour.

Dennis is particularly taken with a fantastic oil painting on a massive scale, displayed in a stairwell. Depicting musical instruments, every attention has been paid to detail, down to the grain of the wood on the violins and the metallic sheen on the wind instruments. It is an outstanding study in textures. Today's special price tag: only forty thousand Euros.

"Wrap it up, I'll take two," Dennis quips.

The Director's still smiling. Hopefully, she doesn't understand.

We're back in the plush room with the Venetian sunset. If money were no object…

"If you want that one you can pay in instalments of one hundred Euros per month over three years, interest free. The initial deposit will be nine hundred Euros." The Director is sitting at the bureau, working figures out with a calculator.

Attempting to save face, I explain that we have a problem.

"It's difficult because I would like this one but I know my husband prefers the oil painting of instruments. We need to talk together and reach an agreement."

"Well, as I said, the exhibition finishes today but I can give you to the end of the week to make up your mind. Here is my phone number." She hands me a printed business card.

We retrieve our coats and, promising to be in touch, make a speedy exit.

That was nearly another fine mess we got us

into. I heave a great sigh of relief as we gear ourselves up to cope with the Public Writer.

*

The Public Writer is a new concept to me. To help those who haven't a clue how to write a bureaucratic letter (me, for instance) the Mairie provides a free service (by appointment, of course) with someone familiar with French bureaucracy and the formal language required to deal with it.

In my case, although I now speak fluent colloquial French, it's quite a different matter when it comes to writing an official letter to increase the standing order for the quarterly charges on my apartment. I tried to change the amount over the Post Office counter but hit the buffers – it can only be done by written request – and of course, the assistant couldn't possibly do it for me. She did, however, suggest the Public Writer.

So here I am at the Mairie, sitting in a large waiting room with ten minutes before my meeting. Dennis, who's happy to leave this to me, is playing a game on his mobile phone. He's a big kid at heart but at least it'll keep him quiet and content whilst I attend to adult things!

A woman in a black suit strides towards us, carrying a pile of paperwork. I half rise to my feet but she veers off into an office.

It's two minutes to four. A young woman with a bouquet breezes in. The Receptionist kisses her on both cheeks, takes her to another office and pulls down a blind.

Four o'clock. A shabbily dressed old woman enters, pulling a shopping trolley with one hand and a tiny shitzu puppy on a lead with the other. She's heading in our direction. I hope her appointment doesn't clash with mine.

"Monsieur et Madame Fielding?" she enquires.

"Oui," I reply hesitantly. Surely she can't be the Public Writer?

But as she introduces herself, asking us to accompany her to her office, she takes on an air of authority, dispelling any doubt. So much for first impressions!

We sit facing her across a desk.

The Public Writer dumps her trolley in a corner, switches on her computer and talks quietly to her little dog, giving him a biscuit.

In French I explain my difficulty. She makes notes on a pad.

"I shall deal with this," she responds kindly. "But I must first make an important call."

I watch her dial a number on her mobile and feel like an eavesdropper as she discusses, presumably with her doctor, the medical tests she requires before her forthcoming operation.

"I have a heart problem," she explains, putting the phone on her desk.

I make sympathetic noises as she consults her computer, muttering under her breath.

"Merde alors!" she exclaims. "The number I need is not in the Yellow Pages. I'll have to phone the local Post Office. Please give me your standing order and account details." She sounds irritated.

She dials a number on her desk phone.

Now there's a heated argument with an official. Even bureaucrats have trouble with bureaucrats!

Slamming down the receiver she composes herself and turns to me.

This is perhaps not the best time to mention that her pet is chewing at my sandal strap.

"Relief for us both at last!" she says. "I can now write your letter."

She types with two fingers on her computer, chuntering to herself.

"There!" She prints off the letter, which she gets me to sign, puts it in an envelope, addresses it and gives it to me.

"All you have to do is put on a stamp."

"Could I please have a copy? Then I won't have to bother you in future."

She obliges, hands it to me flamboyantly and scoops up her dog.

"Au revoir, Madame et Monsieur!"

My next bank statement will show if I've successfully jumped through yet another French bureaucratic hoop…

At the bus stop a prowling pack of uniformed inspectors pounces on passengers exiting a bus. Two check tickets while three watch, probably on the lookout for anyone trying to slip away unnoticed.

I approach an inspector and innocently relate this morning's incident with my Navigo pass.

"Why wouldn't the barrier open?" I want to know.

"Because you used it more than once in quick succession, Madame. You can't have heard it bleep the first time. You're lucky I wasn't around because this scanner would have registered a non-payment on your card and I'd have issued an immediate forty Euro fine."

"But what was I supposed to do?" I argue. "There was no station official to ask."

"You should have waited about ten minutes before re-using it," he states matter-of-factly.

I'm still pondering this on the tiresome climb to our apartment.

Struggling to locate my keys I'm startled to hear a man's voice coming from my jacket pocket.

"Allo! Allo!" it's repeating.

"Either your jacket's developed a voice of its own or your phone's trying to tell you something," Dennis says unhelpfully.

My mobile is lit up. I put it to my ear.

"Allo?" I reply.

"How can we help?" a French voice asks politely.

"Who is that?"

"The Police, Madame. You rang our emergency number."

Suddenly I recall that I'd left my phone unlocked. It must somehow have dialled 17.

"I'm sorry, it was accidental." My face is reddening.

"I think I'll go back to bed and start today again," I tell a puzzled Dennis as I open the door.

Chapter *Vingt-Deux*

We're up before the sparrows today.

When my insurance gave the go-ahead for refurbishment last week the decorating firm stepped in to renew the wonky floorboards. It feels good to look at shiny, varnished floors, to walk barefoot on their smooth, flat surface. And today, the walls are going to be painted, in colours they allowed me to choose.

"The painters will be here at eight, Dennis. We must be ready to get out from under their feet like we did last week."

"Don't rush me. I'm enjoying my coffee."

The doorbell rings.

As they come in we slide past them to get out. I give one man the keys, which he'll post in my letterbox when they finish.

We get the bus to the Hotel des Impôts, the local tax office, where I shall have to explain that I'm late paying the Owners' Tax because the bill arrived at our French address instead of the English one where I asked them to send it. Dare I hope my case will be viewed sympathetically?

At Reception I take a ticket from the machine and we wait… and wait. Everyone else here has a resigned look, though what it is they're resigned to I'm not sure. Maybe it's to a long wait or perhaps they're anticipating a battle with the System.

We stare at a screen that displays the number of the current lucky ticket-holder.

'32 SALLE 3'

Bingo! Ticket thirty-two is the one I'm holding.

In room three, facing me across the desk, the black-haired, black-moustached man listens with an expression of carefully practised patience to my long-winded explanation.

"Ok, Madame. What you must do is go to another department in another suburb." He writes down the details for me. "Tell them what you've told me. They are authorised to give you a document that you take to the local Public Treasury to pay your tax."

That wasn't so bad, then. I thank him and return to explain the situation to Dennis.

"But that's miles out of Paris!" Dennis protests. "I thought you said this would take two minutes."

"Well this is France and I was wrong," I reply tersely.

We pause en route to the Métro, drawn by the display in the patisserie window of mouth-watering, exquisitely designed birthday, christening and wedding cakes, some ready sliced in daintily decorated boxes.

I stop salivating long enough to answer my mobile phone.

"Hi Mum. You're not going to believe this."

"Try me," I dare her.

"I've just passed my driving test!" she shrieks painfully into my unwary ear. "And I'm going to look for a car so next time you come out it'll be me collecting you from the station," she promises – or is that a threat?

"Congratulations, darling!" I say, before remembering that she's referring to driving on the wrong side of the road in what for motorists is Maniac City, where the main rule is Survival Of The Fittest. I can only pray that she's among The Fittest.

"The examiner gave me three chances," she continues. "The first two times I got to a junction I was over the line. It was third time lucky."

Lucky for whom? I suppress my horror on hearing this and pass the phone to Dennis, so she can tell him her news. I'm sure she'll make it sound more upbeat than I can.

"Well done, love," he's saying. "Only, don't be in too much of a hurry to buy a car. The transport system here is perfectly – "

He winces at whatever she replies, probably at both the content and volume.

Dennis has turned quite pale.

"I'm pleased for Nikki," I tell him, "but I can't say I'm thrilled at the thought of her picking us up in a car. I'd feel safer in a cardboard box on the edge of a cliff. Perhaps she won't be able to afford –"

"She's got a friend in the motor trade who can get her a cheap deal on a Peugeot," Dennis interrupts. I detect a hint of hysteria in his tone.

He calms himself on the train by using a stopwatch to note the elapsed time between stations. Utterly fascinated by everything Métro, he knows much of its history, can quote every major interchange and proudly recites nine and a half of the sixteen lines without reference to the map.

Whilst I haven't caught the Métro bug as powerfully as Dennis, I am intrigued by the colourful and often artistic graffiti. It's a mystery to me how or why anyone gains access for the considerable time it must take to cover the interior of tunnels along each route, quite apart from the danger involved. And I enjoy revisiting themed stations like Arts et Métiers on Line 11, designed like a submarine with gleaming copper and strategically placed portholes, and Bastille, on Line 1, tiled with flamboyant images from the French Revolution.

As we transfer to a bus I feel thoroughly fed up. This beautiful day is being wasted, trekking everywhere to pay one bill. I ask the driver to let us know when we get to the road we want and he tells us to watch the illuminated sign that informs passengers of the next stop.

We've got off two stops too soon. It's the right road but apparently the tax office is a lot further down. And this neighbourhood isn't even interesting to walk through with its anonymous looking houses and factories.

We've come to the door of the Central Tax Office, an uninspiring piece of architecture that characterises such government buildings everywhere. And it's closed for lunch. Just what we need!

"I'm hungry," I tell Dennis.

"Of course you are," he says. "It's lunchtime. I'm starving. I hope there's somewhere to eat round here."

We explore the locality in hope rather than expectation of a café, a pub, a restaurant…

We happen on a tiny brasserie where they not

only have omelette and chips on the menu, but are happy to serve it. That puts them one up on Picpus! The owner is friendly and the food tasty. Even Dennis is complimentary.

Returning to the now open Tax office, we are sent to the top floor, where a queue is snaking out of a large room along a corridor. Peering inside, we see two officials on duty.

"Prepare for an afternoon's wait," Dennis warns, taking out his Métro map to amuse himself.

*

"Two more hours gone!" Dennis complains. "I'm going to need more than a Métro map to keep me occupied if we have to keep standing around."

"Our bus is coming," I call, breaking into a run. "If we miss this one we'll have a lot more standing around."

We make it just in time. Now for the Public Treasury…

The title of the office may be grand but the actuality is a cramped, prefabricated building filled with the usual queues.

Finally I push my documentation through the glass partition to a poker-faced official, who slams a rubber stamp down on it.

I begin to write my cheque…

"Not here!" she intervenes.

"What do you mean?" I ask sharply.

"This is where you get it stamped. Then you go to the far window to pay."

With admirable self-restraint I resist telling her

that she's the last straw, that her parentage was questionable and where she can stuff the paperwork and her condescending tone, reminding myself that she's simply doing her tedious, bureaucratic job the best she knows how.

My cheque accepted, an official locks the door behind us, wishing us *bonne soirée*. And he's right, we deserve a good evening after a day like this.

Chapter *Vingt-Trois*

I'm pining for Paris, for our little apartment, for the sheer joy of speaking French. Owing to family circumstances we've been unable to visit for seven months.

Now, relaxed in our Eurostar seats, we're experiencing our first trip on the newly opened high-speed line from St Pancras to Gare du Nord. No more struggling across London on overcrowded Tube trains to Waterloo and as an added bonus we reach Paris twenty minutes earlier than on the previous route.

I'm so absorbed in a book that I'm astonished when Dennis informs me that we passed through the Channel Tunnel a long while back and will soon be at our destination. I hadn't even noticed the stop at Lille.

My French mobile rings the second I turn it on. It's weird how Nikki intuitively senses these things. "Mum, I'll have to be quick, I'm running out of credit. Are you on time?"

I assure her that we are and she promises to be waiting at the end of the platform. I'm so grateful she's giving us a ride to the apartment, as throughout France public transport has ground to a halt in yet another politically motivated strike.

Daylight is fading as the train pulls into the station. I feel the familiar childlike buzz of excitement at being back in Paris.

Nikki is waving to us at the exit, her pretty face alight with happiness. We hug and kiss before following her through the lines of people holding up cards with names of passengers they're meeting in.

She's parked several streets away because it's the nearest she could get.

Walking through streets densely packed with heavy traffic, much of it hooting impatiently, Dennis looks as overawed as I feel. Motorbikes, scooters, bicycles without lights and people on skateboards and roller blades negotiate any available space between cars, vans and buses, often ignoring red traffic lights. And pedestrians are everywhere, adding to the chaos.

Nikki appears to be taking it in her stride.

"Apparently," she says, "people are even sleeping on office floors overnight to avoid spending hours travelling each day."

We eventually reach Nikki's red Peugeot that she affectionately calls Mickey -a true Parisian car, complete with designer dents.

Dennis heaves his bulging suitcase and backpack onto the back seat and climbs in beside them, while I get in beside Nikki unencumbered by luggage. My pockets carry all that I need.

She pulls out and somehow, miraculously, joins the barely-moving stream of traffic.

"You did that well," I remark.

"You seize the chance when you can." She's completely unfazed as a motorcycle shoots straight across her path.

"In honour of this taxi ride I've chosen to wear my brown trousers today," Dennis announces, clinging tightly to the back of my seat.

"You'll be fine with me, Dad," Nikki tries to reassure him.

"Yes, I expect I will," he agrees in a strangled voice.

She isn't fooled but makes no comment. I cannot help but admire her ability to drive in conditions like this. How does she remain so calm, so serene faced with every type of vehicle edging in front, behind, alongside and around her? She seems almost to enjoy it, to welcome the challenge it presents.

Is it my imagination or is that the sound of Dennis praying? He must be desperate. Or maybe he's swearing quietly to himself. And I think I need a toilet.

The world suddenly takes on a surreal quality as an old man on a child's scooter passes within inches of us. Near miss follows near miss but Nikki is unperturbed as she negotiates a huge roundabout, nonchalantly describing the traffic's manoeuvres as some kind of dance.

The journey feels interminable.

Suddenly she slows to a stop and we're outside our apartment block. Dennis breathes an audibly dramatic sigh of relief.

"It's taken an hour and a half to get here," He's miraculously regained the power of speech. "Don't think I'm ungrateful or anything but that was as much fun as being poked with a burnt stick."

Nikki and I exchange smiles, familiar with this line.

While Nikki waits in the car, we climb the stairs and do a brief check to reassure ourselves that the apartment has survived intact in our absence. I turn on the electricity and water and use the toilet.

Dennis dumps his luggage in the bedroom.

We rejoin Nikki and she drives the short distance to the town centre where we walk down the still-busy street arguing whether to eat Turkish, Indian or Chinese. Indian wins by a landslide (two to one).

"Mum, watch your purse!" Nikki warns urgently and steers me insistently towards an estate agent's window.

"Pretend you're looking at house prices and don't turn round!" she hisses in my ear.

Out of the corner of my eye I see a hooded figure scurry past. He pauses further up the street.

"He was within inches of you," Dennis whispers.

It's obvious what happened. He must have heard us speaking English, assumed we were tourists and thought he would find good pickings.

We cross the road to avoid him and walk uphill towards the restaurant, crossing back again as we draw level with it.

The man begins to move towards us. I panic and, in my rush to get into the safety of the restaurant, lose my footing. I land painfully on my knees, my head bent low. Looking slowly upwards I find I'm prostrated at the feet of an Indian waiter.

I stand awkwardly, rubbing my knees and attempting to hide my embarrassment at my strange entry.

Glancing behind, I see the hooded figure hurry swiftly past. I'm reminded once again of the need to be vigilant.

As we eat and catch up on each other's news I

gradually unwind and regain my composure.

The meal over, Nikki drives us home, where Dennis and I are soon tucked up beneath our cosy duvet on the mezzanine.

Chapter *Vingt-Quatre*

"It's almost eleven o'clock," I gasp.

Dennis stirs sleepily beside me. We've frequently played the 'who's-going-to-get-up-first-and-make-breakfast?' game. Feeling hungry, I decide it's me today. Will I be doing this when I'm in my eighties, I wonder, on my backwards descent down the ladder.

I go into the lounge and throw open the shutters. Sunshine streams through the windows, warming the entire room. I switch on the heater, although it's really not that cold considering it's nearly the end of November.

Despite our shared love of Paris I've yet to convert Dennis to the French diet so it's tea, toast and marmalade for him and, in an attempt to lose weight, porridge and fruit for me.

After a weekend of trekking as far as our feet will take us locally, we discover that the strike has petered out. So it's back to riding on the Métro, Dennis' favourite method of travel. And since he has developed an excellent geographical knowledge of the city I refer to him for the route to Montparnasse, our agreed destination.

"Line 6 when we reach Nation," he informs me.

On the train I reflect how compact Paris is, how you can travel its complete breadth in less than an hour. Nikki claims to have driven the entire circuit of the Périphérique in twenty-five minutes, though whether or not this was within the legal limit of 80 kilometres (50 miles) per hour I neither know nor will I ask.

Coming out of the exit of the main line Gare de Montparnasse we're confronted with a huge tower, Paris' sole skyscraper. Dennis immediately goes into Guidebook Mode, explaining that many Parisians regard it as being absurdly out of place, a blot on their city's landscape. It can be seen from miles around. Apparently the views of Paris are spectacular from the restaurant, the highest in Europe, though we're not going to verify this for ourselves owing to Dennis' inbuilt vertigo anywhere above ground level, added to which we've heard that drinks are so expensive you need a mortgage for a couple of cups of coffee.

But in any case, this building is not the reason we're here. We're looking for something much smaller, more discreet and harder to find – a secret garden that, according to Dennis' guidebook, no visitor ever discovers by accident. It's called the Jardin de l'Atlantique, presumably because trains from this station go to France's Atlantic coast. The book says it's behind the main entrance to the station and above the railway, something we find hard to visualise. You can enter via either of the side roads alongside the station. We follow the line of the station building but without seeing a garden.

Out of curiosity we follow a ramp that takes us upwards to a cleverly landscaped, full-blown park with a well-equipped play area for children, tennis courts, plenty of seating and a raised wooden walkway circling the area. A small sign tells us that this is what we've been looking for. Every so often there are entrances from the walkway into the park.

And going down one of these we pass a toilet – or rather, I don't, being unable to resist such an opportunity. Most Parisian parks I've been in seem to lack this facility.

"Hang on a minute, Dennis," I call out, diving into what turns out to be a relatively clean convenience.

Emerging, I find him peering through a grating surrounded by railings. Through it we can see trains at platforms below.

"Do you realise that we're actually on the roof of the station?" Dennis exclaims.

I look round at the extensive garden, at its attractive lawns, flowerbeds and trees. What an amazing feat of engineering this is as well as being a place of stillness and beauty!

"We must come back here in spring, Dennis, when everything will be a blaze of colour."

"Yes," he answers absently, looking across the lawn in front of us. "What's that? Looks like some steps leading down. Maybe they go to the station. Let's find out."

I lift a foot. It's poised, ready to step onto the grass.

"Non, Madame! C'est interdit!" The loud, firm voice beside me halts my action mid-air.

How co-incidental that at this very moment a woman in uniform, who I assume is a park attendant, appears out of nowhere. Do they live in the bushes?

I replace my offending foot on the path and pursue my point.

"What are those steps for, then?"

"Pour le parking," she replies.

How she imagines people can access their cars without crossing the grass is a mystery to me.

"*Regardez*," she continues to ram home her message.

I follow the direction of her finger to a board informing us that 'the lawns of this garden are in repose from 15th October to 15 April.' I'm almost tempted to come up here on 16th April and stomp all over the well-rested grass. There's still a lot of the rebel in me. And in Paris there are numerous rules designed to keep the public in order.

Nevertheless, I smile respectfully at the attendant, who returns my smile with the tolerant expression that might be used for a naughty child.

Leaving the garden we return to the front of the station where to one side we discover a glass-panelled lift shaft with a clear sign, way above eye-level, that reads, "Jardin de l'Atlantique." A walkway at the top joins it to the station roof.

So much for a "secret" garden!

"My feet are aching. Let's go home."

But Dennis' need for exploration is not yet satisfied.

"Now we've come this far, let's take Line 6 a bit further. I've heard that much of it's above ground and we might see something interesting. It's somewhere we haven't been. And at least we'll be sitting down."

I follow him into the Métro.

My reluctance fades as we peer down from the train onto busy streets below. Judging from the elegant buildings, neat little parks and pleasant, spacious streets this must be a well-to-do part of Paris, probably off the tourist trail.

As our train moves out of Bir Hakeim station, a remarkable panorama unfolds. The Eiffel Tower, close by, dominates the skyline. Beside it, framed by small ships and pleasure craft, the Seine flows majestically with a magnificently golden, setting sun shimmering on the water. The tower glows richly bronze in the evening light.

For a rare moment, I am speechless. This has to be one of the most marvellous sights anywhere in the city, all the better for being so unexpected and certainly well worth the detour.

Pulling into Passy station on the other side of the river we resolve to return, next time with our cameras.

*

As is my custom on the last evening of my stay, I wander from room to room of the apartment, familiar with every detail of our Cosy Cupboard on the edge of one of the most beautiful cities in the world. Everything in it has its own special story, from that offcut of quality carpet in the shower room, given to me free in Leroy Merlin, to the stepladder that nearly decapitated another passenger on the bus.

I go into the kitchen and watch the setting sun's rays making the sky aglow with colour and illuminating the bright primrose walls.

No matter how problematic life can be, this tiny haven of peace is a priceless refuge. No country mansion, palatial chateau or noble castle could give me such contentment. Never have I felt so gently enveloped, tenderly protected and quietly at home as within the walls of this little apartment.

"While you're in the kitchen, can you put the kettle on," calls Dennis. "I could do with a nice cup of English tea."

Epilogue

I thought long and hard about a title for this book. I came up with "Wrinklies In Paris", "French Bureaucracy And Me" and "How I Bought A Small Apartment In Paris And Learned To Love The French". But nothing seemed to fit and its working title remained "The French Book" – not exactly original but at least it was easy to find on my computer.

I decided to try a different tack. I began to reread the book hoping to come across something appropriate embedded somewhere in the text. After a few pages I found precisely what I was looking for.

"Now I'm about to look for a flat in Paris...
I must be mad!"

I remembered that at this point in my life I had just left a psychiatric hospital following a breakdown. And I also recalled the dreadful joke about the Frenchman jumping off a bridge and being declared In Seine…

Et voilà! My title.

But I've always wanted to give my words the ring of truth…

So here I am with Dennis, beside the great river that divides Paris in two. It's seven o'clock on a winter's evening. I feel very daring, walking down a ramp towards the water in the shadow of the quay wall. We approach the point where the ramp meets the water lapping against its cobbled stones. The street lamps are glinting off the river, giving me sufficient light to see what I'm about to do.

I've come prepared. I ask Dennis for the paper towelling. Quickly, without giving myself a chance to change my mind having come this far, I remove the boot and sock from one foot, take a deep breath and plunge my bare foot into the water.

I thought it would be freezing but it's considerably warmer than the air temperature.

I lean against the wall to dry my foot, feeling a warm glow of achievement.

I've done it! I've finished my book.

Now I can truthfully say I've gone *In Seine*!

3344705R00117

Printed in Great Britain
by Amazon.co.uk, Ltd.,
Marston Gate.